VATICAN II

Vatican II

Did Anything Happen?

JOHN W. O'MALLEY, JOSEPH A.
KOMONCHAK,
STEPHEN SCHLOESSER, AND NEIL J. ORMEROD

Edited by
DAVID G. SCHULTENOVER

continuum

NEW YORK • LONDON

2008

The Continuum International Publishing Group Inc
80 Maiden Lane, New York, NY 10038
The Continuum International Publishing Group Ltd
The Tower Building, 11 York Road, London SE1 7NX

www.continuumbooks.com

Printed in the United States of America

Library of Congress Cataloging-in-Publication Data

Vatican II : did anything happen? / John W. O'Malley ... [et al.] ; edited by David G. Schultenover.
    p. cm.
Includes bibliographical references.
ISBN-13: 978-0-8264-2890-5 (pbk. : alk. paper)
ISBN-10: 0-8264-2890-8 (pbk. : alk. paper)
1. Vatican Council (2nd : 1962-1965) I. O'Malley, John W. II. Schultenover, David G., 1938-
BX8301962 .V3265 2007
262'.52—dc22

                              2007038155

CONTENTS

INTRODUCTION

John W. O'Malley, S.J.

THE SECOND VATICAN COUNCIL ended decades ago, yet the problem of interpreting it is as lively today as it has ever been. The articles collected in this volume address that problem. They are by four different authors, each of whom has a different approach, yet there is a remarkable convergence among them on two crucial points. First, the authors know each other's writings on the council and in an interactive way cross-reference them. The last three were originally published in *Theological Studies*, with the third spinning off the second, and the fourth spinning off the preceding two. The first appeared earlier and separately but, as reading it will make clear, it belongs here with the others. The articles are thus four interlocutors in a constructive conversation. They all deal with the fundamental interpretative questions: Did anything of significance happen at the council? If so, what? So what? And, finally, what methods will help answer these questions?

There is a second and more specific point of convergence. All four articles deal with the impact of history on the Church and on the council and thus deal with the problem of change. How continuous or discontinuous was the council with previous councils, with previous teachings and practices? As will become clear in the articles themselves, today a strong, and at least semiofficial, interpretation of the council insists in such an exclusive way on the council's continuity with the Catholic past that it seems to minimize the council's significance. This interpretation seems to our authors to remove the council (and the Church) from its historical contexts and even from the historical process itself. The articles take on that interpretation and in different ways challenge it.

In this introduction I want to provide background to help readers toward a fuller appreciation of what the articles are getting at and, in so doing, I write more for someone beginning to study the council than for experts. I provide, therefore, basic information about the origins of the council, the issues it dealt with, and the larger contexts into which it must be situated. With that information behind them, readers are ready to jump into the articles themselves, which are best read in the order they appear.

The Council

On January 25, 1959, Pope John XXIII announced, to everyone's astonishment, his intention of convoking an ecumenical council. After the First Vatican Council (1869–1870), many theologians and historians had speculated that, with its definitions of papal primacy and papal infallibility, councils had become superfluous in the Church—the pope could solve all problems. John XXIII's announcement obviously proved them wrong. It has meanwhile become known that in the early 1920s Pius XI and again in the early 1950s Pius XII considered calling a council to resume and complete Vatican I, which had been interrupted when the troops of the new Italian nation seized Rome. But by 1959 those initiatives were well guarded secrets, and it is not clear that John XXIII knew of them before he made his announcement. He consistently maintained that the idea had come to him spontaneously and as an inspiration.

But a council to do what? The pope made no mention of Vatican I, and he never seems to have considered the council he envisaged as a resumption of it. In any case, he put all doubts to rest on the matter when on July 14 he informed Cardinal Domenico Tardini, the Vatican's secretary of state, that the council would be called Vatican II. This meant it would be a new council and therefore would not have to carry out, even in revised forms, the unfinished agenda of the earlier one. It could pursue its own path.

But what was that path to be? Of the 20 councils the Catholic Church at that point recognized as ecumenical, the better known, like the Council of Trent (1545–1563), had been convoked to deal with a crisis. Although as the preparations for Vatican II got under way and serious issues began to emerge, in 1959 no obvious crisis was troubling the Catholic Church. In fact, except in those parts of the world where Christianity was undergoing overt persecution, mainly in countries under Communist domination, the Church in the decade and a half since the end of World War II gave evidence of vigor and self-confidence.

Why, then, a council, and what was it supposed to do? In his announcement on January 15 John XXIII mentioned, almost in passing, two aims that were tantalizingly vague. The first was to promote "the enlightenment, edification, and joy of the entire Christian people," and the second was to extend "a renewed cordial invitation to the faithful of the separated churches to participate with us in this feast of grace and brotherhood."[1] These aims could be dismissed as pious generalities, and they more than suggest that at this point John XXIII himself had little clarity about the specifics with which the council might deal. Nonetheless, they were remarkable for two reasons.

First, the announced aims were couched in altogether positive terms. Especially from the beginning of the 19th century up until John's pontificate, the popes and offices of the Holy See framed public statements not always but most characteristically in negative terms of warning or condemnation, and even when proposing a positive measure did so to provide an antidote to "the evils of the times." The significance of this fact would become clear only later, in the light of some of John XXIII's subsequent statements and especially in the light of his allocution on October 11, 1962, opening the council. These positive terms adumbrated the approach he would consistently commend for the council.

The second announced aim extended a hand in friendship to the other Christian churches, and it did so, it seemed, without strings attached. The invitation was not "to return" but "to participate." In his heart of hearts John, like all Catholics of that time, was probably harboring hopes that the council might lead to a "return," but, for whatever reason, he did not thus express himself. From the very beginning, the council had its eyes turned in part to persons outside the parameters of the Roman Catholic Church, whom it wanted to meet in "brotherhood." The pope's "invitation" was a gentle but significant departure from the papal policy of eschewing ecumenical encounters, a policy that had been strongly reaffirmed and insisted on by Pius XI in his encyclical *Mortalium animos* (1928) and asserted in less stringent terms by Pius XII as late as 1950 in his encyclical *Humani generis*.

Preparations for the council moved in two distinct phases. The first opened in May 1959 with the appointment of a so-called prior-to-preparation ("antepreparatory") commission whose task was to gather opinions from bishops and others about issues needing action. The results of this consultation provided the materials for the second phase, the "preparatory" phase properly speaking, during which those materials were shifted, organized, and formulated into texts to be presented to the council when it opened. Although the antepreparatory commission originally planned to send a questionnaire, Pope John indicated he wanted only a letter to be sent, presumably because it would be less prejudicial to what would be discussed. The letter exhorted the addressees to offer their ideas "with complete freedom and honesty . . . on anything that you think is good to discuss and clarify."[2] The letter went to 2,598 ecclesiastics and elicited 1,998 (77%) responses. Later the congregations of the Roman Curia and institutions of higher learning around the world that held papal charters were asked to do the same.

By and large, the responses called for a tightening of the status quo, for condemnations of modern evils whether inside or outside the Church, and for some further definitions of doctrine, especially relating to the Virgin Mary. A few were more venturesome, particularly in asking for greater responsibility for the laity in the Church and extension of the use of the vernacular in the Mass, despite Pius XII's recent cautions in that regard. By the spring of 1960 all the responses had arrived, and preparations moved into the second phase.

• Pope John then set up ten commissions to compose documents on subjects that had emerged from the consultation. These commissions were headed by cardinals who, with one exception, were prefects of a Vatican congregation. A central Coordinating Commission was to oversee the work of the others. Besides these commissions, the pope established a Secretariate for Christian Unity, whose original task was restricted to not much more than simple liaison with other Christian bodies but, once the council was under way, was given the status of a full commission. The commissions worked for two years to produce documents that they hoped the council would accept after a minimum of discussion and amendment. The commissions worked with varying degrees of intensity, with greater or lesser recourse to the results of the consultation, and with little coordination from the Coordinating Commission. The commissions produced a whopping 70 documents!

Even with that number of items on the agenda, some bishops still grasped at the unlikely prospect the council would be able to accomplish its business in one session. As it turned out four sessions were required, each of which, held in the fall, lasted about ten weeks, 1962–1965. On June 3, 1963, Pope John died of stomach cancer, and the council went forward under his successor, Paul VI. There were many reasons why the council lasted so long, including sometimes ineffectual rules of procedure, but the main reason was the council's substantive reworking of the material it originally received and even a rejection of important parts of it. Drama therefore marked every session of the council, as the debate between those who identified with the orientations of the original documents clashed with those who opposed them. The latter group emerged much the stronger— somewhere between 85 and 90 percent of the participants, depending on the issue under consideration.

By the time the council concluded, Paul VI had promulgated in his name and in the name of the council—"Paul, bishop, together with the council"—16 documents, a considerable reduction from the original 70. They cover an extraordinarily wide range of subjects and do so at considerable length. They are the council's most authoritative and accessible legacy, and it is around them that study of the council must obviously turn. These documents, however, breathe an air of serenity that obscures the fact that some of them were hotly, often bitterly, contested in the council and survived only by the skin of their teeth.

That air of serenity also obscures the general issues that underlay and gave rise to the specific issues, and thus obscures what, deep down, the council was wrestling with. These deep-down issues are with us still; they will not go away. They are issues that acutely agitated the council, even though the bishops may not have been able to articulate them for themselves with the clarity that hindsight provides. The articles in this volume try to provide that articulation.

Interpreters of the council who insist almost exclusively on the continuity of the council with the Catholic tradition, and thus give it a minimal interpretation, base their case on two principles. First, the meaning of the council is to be found in the final documents, and, as they correctly maintain, in those documents there is no indication of any break with the past or any suggestion of a change from "business as usual."

The documents are the products of the largest committee in the history of the world, some 2,300 bishop—full, therefore, of compromises and euphemisms. Moreover, in the council itself, minimizing suggestions of change served the purposes of all parties. It served the purposes of the so-called progressives (the substantial majority) in that those bishops argued that what they were proposing was a genuine expression of the tradition, not the aberration or heresy that the so-called conservatives (the minority) labeled those proposals. Once the hoped-for changes had won overwhelming approval in the council, the minority party wanted to minimize the damage by also giving the impression that no change was occurring.

The second principle on which the minority party insisted is "that's it!"—no need to look beyond the documents. No need to look to the contexts out of which they grew, which means no need to study any "before" or "after" or to examine the documents beyond their surface statements. In effect what this principle implies is the lifting of the council out of history and, by focusing exclusively on the wording of the documents, making them into a textbook of abstract, perennial teachings.

What are those 16 documents? Although they are often lumped together without distinction of rank, they theoretically were not equal in dignity or in the authority to be attributed to them. The highest in rank were the "constitutions," of which there were only four: the documents on the liturgy (*Sacrosanctum concilium*), on the Church (*Lumen gentium*), on divine revelation (*Dei verbum*), and on the Church in the modern world (*Gaudium et spes*). The other documents are to be interpreted in conformity with the principles and directions enunciated in these constitutions.

Next in rank came nine so-called "decrees": on the communications media (*Inter merifica*), on the Catholic Eastern churches (*Orientalium ecclesiarum*), on ecumenism (*Unitatis redintegratio*), on bishops (*Christus Dominus*), on religious orders (*Perfectae caritatis*), on the training of priests (*Optatam totius*), on the life and ministry of priests (*Presbyterorum ordinis*), on missionary activity (*Ad gentes divinitus*), and on the apostolate of the laity (*Apostolicam actuositatem*). Finally, there were three "declarations": on Christian education (*Gravissimum educationis*), on non-Christian religions (*Nostra aetate*), and on religious liberty and church–state relations (*Dignitatis humanae*).

If these 16 documents differ in rank, they differ more palpably in impact and practical importance. The constitutions have managed to consolidate their theoretical importance by the attention, scrutiny, and, for the most part, the positive appreciation they have consistently received from scholars. But the distinction between decrees and declarations, no matter what it originally meant, has become meaningless, with the decrees on the communications media, for instance, and on the Eastern churches practically forgotten, whereas the declarations on religious liberty and on non-Christian religions are just as important as they were during the council.

The Issues

The scope of the issues the council addressed is almost breathtaking. It dealt with: the use of the organ in church services, the legitimacy or illegitimacy of stockpiling nuclear weapons, the place of Thomas Aquinas in seminary curricula, how priests are to be financially compensated for their services, with the purposes of marriage, translations of the Bible, the role of conscience in moral decision-making, worshiping with non-Catholics, and so on—almost, it might seem, into infinity.

- All the issues must be taken seriously, but some are certainly of greater significance. Generally speaking, the most important issues were the most contested on the floor of the council and ignited the most spectacular verbal fireworks. The fireworks almost invariably exploded when the proposition under consideration was perceived by some as so deviating from previous practice or teaching as to be "inopportune" or "dangerous" or "illegitimate" or maybe even "heretical." The time and effort spent on an issue was almost invariably in direct proportion to the measure's perceived degree of violation of received teaching—in the view of some bishops, and often enough that teaching had been expressed in a papal document of the previous 150 years.

- The first issue protractedly debated was the place of Latin in the liturgy. It occupied the council for several weeks. The issue, though important in its own right, had deeper ramifications. It was a first awkward wrestling with the question of the larger direction the council should take: confirm the status quo or move beyond it? The status quo for Latin had seemingly been fixed in stone since the Reformation when all the Protestant churches opted for the vernacular. The council resolved the question of Latin by taking a moderate, somewhat ambiguous position, which got trumped after the council by the most basic principle the council adopted on the liturgy: the insistence on the full and active participation of the whole assembly in the liturgical action.

- Few issues sparked such bitter controversy both inside the council and outside it in the media as the relationship of the Church to the Jews and then to other non-Christian religions. Few of the documents, that is to say, bumped along on such a rough road as did the declaration *Nostra aetate*. The sticking point was relationship to the Jews, and there the burning question was how responsible they were for the death of Jesus. Were the Jews (seemingly as a race) "perfidious," as the prayer for them in the Good Friday liturgy had for centuries described them?

- More pertinent to life in the United States was the rough rode traveled by the document on ecumenism, on the relationship of the Catholic Church to other Christian churches and communions. Since the Reformation the Church had drawn firm lines of demarcation between itself and the other churches, a line reinforced by provisions of the 1917 Code of Canon Law and eleven years later by Pius XI's encyclical *Mortalium animos*. Catholics were forbidden, for instance, to attend a funeral, even of a friend or relative, if it was held in a Protestant church. They were forbidden to attend non-Catholic colleges without the personal permission of the bishop. In a Catholic hospital those in charge were not to call a minister to assist a dying person who was a Protestant.

- The decree on religious liberty traveled a similarly difficult path. Its advocacy of forms of separation of church and state, its insistence that everyone has a right to worship according to one's conscience, and the primacy it gave to conscience over obedience to external authority, aroused fierce opposition because, among other things, the decree seemed to contradict the repeated condemnations by recent popes of separation of church and state. Those of us living in North America do not fully appreciate how radical this document sounded in many parts of the world. Recall that at the time of the council Generalísimo Francisco Franco of Spain had an important voice in the appointment of Spanish bishops, a right of the head of the Spanish state that was not renounced until 1975, by King Juan Carlos. Since the council Popes Paul VI, John Paul II, and Benedict XVI have publically proclaimed the principle of religious liberty as a fundamental human right, yet such a proclamation was inconceivable before 1965.

The decree on the Church prepared before the council was in effect rejected at the end of the first session, December 1962, and sent back to committee for what amounted to such a thorough revision that what emerged was a virtually new document, *Lumen gentium*. The document met criticism on many points and underwent significant revision. No issue turned out to be more contentious than the relationship of the episcopacy to the papacy as contained in the doctrine of collegiality, that is, that the bishops as a college have a responsibility, along with the pope, for the universal Church. A minority in the council passionately opposed this teaching as an infringement on the prerogatives of the papacy as defined at Vatican I.

• The proponents of collegiality found a basis for it in the New Testament, of course, but their model was the church of the first millennium, before the development of the so-called papal monarchy. There were, according to them, two venerable traditions in the church: the special leadership of the bishop of Rome and the authority of other bishops especially when assembled in a synod and most especially when assembled in an ecumenical council. Collegiality was an attempt to bring up out of the past a better pattern for the exercise of authority in the Church.

The Historical Contexts

The aforementioned issues were among the more important up-front issues at the council. What were the historical contexts out of which they developed? The first context pays homage to "*la longue durée*," the ongoing impact of events that happened many centuries ago, such as the deep roots of the church–state issue stretching all the way back to the fourth century and the Emperor Constantine. Church and state at that time were so closely wedded that Constantine not only called the Council of Nicea (325) but also made its decrees the law of the Roman Empire. From that time forward a partnership between secular authorities and the hierarchy persisted in the church through many different forms and vicissitudes. Even as Vatican II was being prepared, the Supreme Congregation of the Holy Office held adamantly to the position that in Catholic countries the state had an obligation to profess and favor the Catholic faith and to limit the practice of all other faiths.

With John XXIII's invitation to other Christian bodies to participate in the council and with the acceptance of the invitation by many of them, the Reformation (as well as the schism of 1059 with the Eastern Orthodox) obviously formed much of the backdrop to the council. How could the Catholic Church now receive as brothers and sisters those whom, until the council opened, it had regarded as heretics. The decrees of the Council of Trent thus came under new scrutiny during the council and entered critically into the debates over ecumenism—as well as into debates over other matters, such as the relationship of Scripture to tradition in the document on revelation.

The more immediate context for the council, however, was "modernity" or, concretely, "the long 19th century," understood as the period stretching, for the Catholic Church, from the French Revolution until the end of the pontificate of Pius XII in 1958. It was a century in which the Church at its grass roots rebounded from the devastations of the French Revolution. In France itself, the Church, despite having to struggle against powerful political and ideological adversaries, flourished. In the Church around the world religious orders of men and women, which were practically extinct by 1800, grew at an astounding rate. Missionaries from Europe arrived in Asia and Africa in unprecedented numbers, often supported openly or covertly by the governments of their native countries. Although in Europe Catholics were opposed to the intellectual mainstream, some significant thinkers emerged, and the seed was sown for important movements that would bear fruit in the council.

Nonetheless, ecclesiastical leadership, especially the papacy, felt itself beleaguered and on the defensive. The French Revolution, with its destruction of churches and its execution of priests, nuns, and the monarch himself, had been a traumatic experience, in some ways more traumatic than the Reformation, for it erupted in Catholic France with its ripple effects felt most keenly in other Catholic countries like Spain, Portugal, and the different political units of Italy. In the Papal States, that immense swath of territory on the Italian peninsula under papal government since the early Middle Ages stretching almost from Naples to Venice, helped create a political crisis that culminated with the seizure of the States by the Risorgimento (1860–1870), the forces working for the unification of Italy. The Holy See regarded that seizure as illegitimate and, with a diminishing degree of insistence, continued to agitate for the restoration to papal rule of at least the city of Rome until 1929 when the controversy was settled by a concordat with Mussolini's government establishing Vatican City as a sovereign state. Not only had the Revolution shaken and temporarily abolished the monarchies on the Continent, but, in so doing, it had also shaken to its foundation the principle of state support of the Catholic Church to the exclusion of all other churches.

Even more devastating was the ideology that carried these events forward. Behind the Revolution lay the Enlightenment, which on the continent was rabidly anticlerical and for the most part anti-Christian, that is, anti-Catholic. "Modernity" is a handy catchword for summing up what was at stake. The thinkers of the Enlightenment turned their backs on the past, turned their faces resolutely to the future, and looked forward to ever better things to come. Among those things was a new era of liberty, equality, and fraternity. Religion and monarchy would no longer shackle the human spirit. No more religious dogma, for Reason was the only god to be adored. The name by which such passionately held views were commonly known in the 19th century was Liberalism. Especially for the papacy Liberalism stood for all that was wrong with the modern world.

Liberalism had to be answered. Culture wars of the first order broke out. The search for responses to this enemy as well as for other problems arising in a society that seemed to be hurtling along with unprecedented speed helped generate one of the most important, yet little commented upon, changes in the papacy in the past millennium. The popes, whose job description regarding doctrine had traditionally been that of a judge, now became teachers. As the principal vehicle for their teaching, the popes created the encyclical. Indicative of the growing importance of the genre is the increased use popes made of it. From the two issued at the end of the 18th century by Pope Pius VI over the course of a pontificate of 24 years and the one by his successor over 23 years, we move to 38 by Pius IX and, by the end of the century, to 75 by Leo XIII. The encyclicals committed the popes to an increasingly large number of positions on a wide range of issues. To what extent could these positions later be changed—positions like Gregory XVI's condemnation in 1832 of freedom of conscience, Pius XI's condemnation in 1930 of birth control, and many popes' condemnation of separation of church and state?

As a consequence of the proliferation of encyclicals, expectations grew among Catholics that one looked to "Rome" for answers to all questions, not only in the more traditional way as to a court of final appeal but as to a teacher with a position on all questions. Besides the encyclicals, decrees of the Roman congregations began to increase in number, as a process of ever more centralized authority grew. The invention of the telegraph and the telephone facilitated this development and was part and parcel of the increasingly determining role the papacy was assuming in Catholic life.

An important milestone was canon 329 in the 1917 Code of Canon Law. The canon affirmed that the pope appoints bishops in the Church. Although the Holy See continued to respect the provisions of concordats and long-standing local traditions that qualified that bald assertion, this canon marked the definitive abandonment of the traditional principle of the free election of bishops, for which the popes had at times fought so bitterly. Ultramontanism, as this tendency to promote papal authority and prerogatives is known, began more and more to define what it meant to be a Roman Catholic. Even as the Liberals touted the end of monarchy, the papacy insisted more and more on its monarchical character, the guarantor of order in a topsy-turvy world.

Besides the emergence of an aggressive Liberalism, another challenge to the Church was the new enthusiasm for historical approaches to almost every academic discipline. This development was long in the making, but it blossomed in the 19th century as never before, with scholars boasting of new methods that gradually moved the discipline of history from its older base in rhetoric and moral philosophy to more controlled methods of research that at a certain point began to be described as "scientific." The method professed objectivity in evaluating evidence and freedom from contamination by apologetic concerns and by what the maintenance of received opinions might require. History was no longer an edifying tale celebrating past achievements or deploring past failures. It strove to be a critical discipline that analyzed the past especially in terms of change that explained the present.

This development, of course, affected Catholic scholarship. Some Catholic historians emerged with prominence, such as Johannes Jansen, Johann Ignaz von Döllinger, and Lord Acton, but the greatest lights were German Lutherans, French and Italian Liberals, and others who were unfavorably disposed toward the Catholic Church. Try as they might to be objective, many historians operated out of assumptions about religion and Christianity that made it difficult for them to appreciate Catholicism and that at times made them downright hostile.

Since the 16th century, moreover, Catholic historical writing emphasized the continuity of the Church with its past, whereas Protestant or Liberal historians were just as obsessed with discontinuities. Luther, Calvin, and other Reformers hurled at the Church the accusation that it was so discontinuous with the past that it had perverted the gospel message. Catholics responded with vehement denials and worked, as the documents of Trent show, to prove that what the Church did and taught was essentially identical with the apostolic age. These two historiographical traditions, in extreme and in modified forms, persisted strong into the 20th century and in some circles up to the present. The one focused on change, the other on continuity, sometimes to the point of denying that any important change had taken place.

In the 19th century a major crisis occurred with the definition of papal infallibility. Döllinger saw the definition as flying in the face of the historical record. When, after the council, he refused to accept the definition, he was excommunicated by the archbishop of Munich. Döllinger led into schism numerous German Catholic intellectuals, of whom the largest single group were historians. In the wake of this crisis and in response to an attack on the definition by the chancellor of Germany, Otto von Bismark, the German bishops issued a statement that the definitions of Vatican I had changed nothing in the tradition of the Church, "not the least thing."[3]

Even more threatening than the work of church historians was the application of the new methods to the most sacred text of all, the Bible. David Friedrich Strauss of the University of Tübingen was more a disciple of Hegel than a historian or exegete, but in 1835 his life of Jesus, *Leben Jesu*, appeared. In it he denied the historical foundation of all supernatural elements in the Gospels. The book, roundly denounced by Protestant and Catholic clergy, created a sensation. Despite its glaring faults, it could not be ignored, and the discussion that swirled around it deeply affected subsequent biblical scholarship.

Some 20 years later came from Catholic France another life of Jesus from a former seminarian, Joseph Ernest Renan. This *Vie de Jésus* similarly rejected the possibility of supernatural elements in the story of Jesus and portrayed him simply as a charming Galilean preacher. Other scholars made use of the same historical, archeological, and philological approaches but came to far less radical conclusions. Among them was Marie-Joseph Lagrange, a French priest of the Dominican order, who, after philological studies at the University of Vienna, in 1890 almost single-handedly founded l'École Biblique, an important center of biblical studies in Jerusalem; it is still functioning today. Although controversy dogged Lagrange's steps, he emerged in learned circles as the leading Catholic exegete.

Advocacy among Catholics of the adoption of the new historical criticism became part of an amorphous and much broader phenomenon that came to be know as "Modernism." The term originated in 1904 with Umberto Benigni, a minor official of the papal curia who, besides being an ardent monarchist, was an archenemy of every philosophical and historical approach that did not fit with his ultraconservative presuppositions. The term could not have come from a more hostile source. From the very beginning the spin Benigni gave the term prejudiced the understanding of what was at stake and almost hopelessly confused the issues.

This confusion explains why the so-called Modernists differed so much among themselves that it is difficult to find a common thread linking them except their desire to help the Church reconcile itself with what they felt was best in intellectual culture as it had evolved into the present. A premise of the movement (if it can be called that) to which they belonged was the pervasiveness of change and the need to reckon with it, though this premise did not have a determining role in the thought of all the Modernists.

The storm broke on July 3, 1907. On that day the Supreme Congregation of the Holy Office issued the decree *Lamentabili*, which formulated and condemned 65 pronouncements supposedly held by the Modernists. Among them, for instance, was no. 11, which denied that the Bible was inspired to the extent that every part of it was utterly free from error, and no. 44, which asserted that marriage evolved as a sacrament only later in Christian history. Two months later, Pius X promulgated his encyclical *Pascendi dominici gregis*, in which he depicted the situation as especially grave because "the partisans of error" are to be found not among the Church's enemies but "in her very heart and bosom." In view of Modernism's thoroughgoing perversity, the pope asserted, the movement was not so much a heresy as "the synthesis of all heresies." The gravity of the evil required drastic measures to uproot it. Anybody found, for instance, "to be imbued with Modernism" as well as anybody found "criticizing scholasticism, the Holy Father, . . . [or showing] a love of novelty in history, archeology, or biblical exegesis" was to be excluded "without compunction" from all teaching positions.[4]

For the sweep of its denunciations, the accusatory style of its language, and especially for the severity of its provisions, *Pascendi* had few, if any, precedents in documents emanating from the papacy. A veritable purge of the Church's intellectuals followed. No doubt, some of the tenets of some of the Modernists could only with difficulty be squared with Christian belief, but in the wake of the encyclical the innocent also got stigmatized and their careers ruined. The definition of Modernism became so general, virtually equated with "any novelty," that it could be applied to almost any serious work of historical scholarship.

Two years after *Lamentabili* and *Pascendi*, Pius founded in Rome the Pontifical Biblical Institute modeled somewhat on l'École Biblique in Jerusalem but intended at least in part as a conservative counterweight to it. With that aim, he entrusted it to the Jesuits and gave it authority to grant ecclesiastical degrees. For some years the "Biblicum," as it is generally known, lived up to the conservative hopes Pius placed in it, but bit by bit the professors had to come to terms with the new methods and use them. In that regard they represent a pattern in Catholic "sacred studies" that would be verified in every field.

Thus the liturgical movement that had gained so much strength by the middle of the 20th century and that led to the changes in worship initiated by Vatican II could not have had a more conservative origin. Prosper Guéranger, Benedictine monk and zealous ultramontanist, was a key figure, representative of the generations that, after the French Revolution, felt a heavy duty to repair the ravages. In 1833 he refounded the monastery of Solesmes in France. He reached an international audience with his immensely important publications, especially *L'Année liturgique*, a nine-volume devotional commentary on the feasts and solemnities of the church year published from 1841 to 1866 and appearing in English translation in 1861 to 1871; it remained popular into the middle of the next century. Guéranger's object was to make the official liturgy of the Church—the Mass and the liturgical hours—the center of worship rather than other services and devotions like novenas that had proliferated in Catholicism since the late Middle Ages.

Monasteries more or less modeled on or inspired by Solesmes sprang up in Belgium, Germany, and elsewhere, including North America, where the Benedictine monastery in Collegeville, Minnesota, would be especially important in the movement. They revived the notion of the monk-scholar whose life outside the time spent celebrating the liturgy was spent on the study of texts, which made some monks formidable historical scholars, not always unaffected by the new methods. As the texts were studied, the patristic period began to replace the Middle Ages as the more normative model for a reform of the liturgy.

By the middle of the 20th century the idea was widespread among scholars that changes were called for. The growing pressure for change led in 1947 to Pius XII's encyclical *Mediator Dei*, in which the pope gave his blessing, not unreserved, to the idea. The pope took seriously the implications of his encyclical and within a few years began to make changes in liturgical practice, the most important of which was the substantial reorganization of the liturgies for the Sacred Triduum, the last three days of Holy Week. This reform entailed, among other things, moving the liturgies for Holy Thursday and Holy Saturday from early morning to evening. Historical scholarship on the liturgy thus had a palpable impact on decision-making at the highest level.

Decades before Leo XIII published *Aeterni Patris* in 1879 decreeing Thomas Aquinas and, with him, the Scholastic system as normative for Catholic theology, Jacques-Paul Migne, a diocesan priest and publishing entrepreneur, was busy in Paris bringing forth monumental editions of different kinds of ecclesiastical texts. None of these editions could compare in impact with his *Patrologia*. Divided into two parts, the *Patrologia latina* (1844–1864), a corpus of Latin writings by Christian authors from the second to the early 13th century, ran to 221 volumes. The *Patrologia graeca* (1856–1866), the corresponding corpus of Greek writings, ran to 162 volumes. For the first time scholars had at their disposal in easily accessible form a magnificent range of authors and texts, many of which they earlier could have consulted only in partial and widely scattered selections. Now every library of substance possessed these texts not as rare books stored carefully away but sitting on open shelves.

Nothing was more important than Migne's *Patrologia* in promoting the study of the church fathers from this time forward. As that study was pursued, the discrepancies in style, focus, and even content between patristic and Scholastic theology became ever clearer and reached a point of special acuity in the middle of the 20th century in France with "la nouvelle théologie." As early as 1947 the Jesuit theologian Henri de Lubac sounded the call for the "return to the sources," the *ressourcement* advocated by the "new" theologians: "Let us abide by the outlook of the Fathers."[5]

One of the first great monuments of patristic scholarship, published in 1833, long before Migne's editions, was *The Arians of the Fourth Century* by a young Anglican divine, John Henry Newman. His research alerted him to the difference between patristic positions on dogmatic matters and the 19th-century teachings of the churches, including Roman Catholicism. His conversion to Catholicism in 1845 was followed almost immediately by his *Essay on the Development of Doctrine* in which, by using different analogies, he tried to show how teachings evolved while remaining fundamentally true to their origins. The book, still the classic on the subject, is ironical in that the thinking behind it led Newman into a Church that on the official level was denying that such evolution took place. In any case, it put the problem of change on the stage of theological debate to a degree unknown before, where it remained to become a central point of contention at Vatican II—and therefore of our volume.

By the eve of Vatican II the problem for Catholicism of historical approaches to sacred subjects was made acute by the proliferation of important studies done from a historical perspective. In 1955, for instance, Brian Tierney published his *Foundations of Conciliar Theory* in which he showed, among other things, that in the Middle Ages mainline canonists assumed that responsibility for the good of the church was distributed among various offices and corporations, each of which had its own intrinsic (not delegated) authority. He implicitly demonstrated that the "conciliarism" that saved the papacy at the Council of Constance at the time of the Great Western Schism could not automatically be identified with the conciliarism that later postulated that a council was in every instance superior in authority to the pope.

The historical approach made inroads into the Neo-Thomist movement through several important German, Belgian, and French scholars. Among them was, for instance, Étienne Gilson. In 1919 he published his first book on Aquinas to begin a long and brilliant career of studies on aspects of medieval philosophy and theology that showed its diversity and historical development. Ten years later he helped found a center in Toronto that in 1939 became the Pontifical Institute of Mediaeval Studies, where historical methods were applied to every facet of medieval life. Meanwhile another development was gaining ground. In 1922 the Belgian Jesuit Joseph Maréchal came out with his five-volume *La pointe de départ de la metaphysique*, which launched an influential movement soon known as Transcendental Thomism. Maréchal opened the door to a more subject-oriented and more historically sensitive theology. He made possible even for Thomists an appropriation of a phenomenologist like Martin Heidigger, who took as his starting point the human person as existing in time and history and as concerned for what that situation means for life's choices. At the time of Vatican II Karl Rahner was the best known exponent of Transcendental Thomism.

Writing at the same time as Maréchal was the Jewish philosopher
and religious thinker Martin Buber, who early on challenged the
objective and impersonal frame of reference in which Western philosophy addressed even human issues. He later went on to criticize
Aristotle and Aquinas for the abstract character of their systems that
removed individuals from real-life situations where they are faced
with choices: "Aquinas knows no special problem and no special
problematic of human life, such as Augustine experienced and expressed with trembling heart."[6] For the abstractions of the great
philosophical systems, Buber substituted relationships in which mu-
tuality and the sharing of experience and beliefs were the hallmarks.
In such relationships the privileged form of communication is dialogue, "conversation . . . from one open-hearted person to another
open-hearted person."[7] In Buber dialogue is not a ploy or technique
but the surface expression of a core value. His writings attracted a
wide readership and directly and indirectly influenced Catholic
thinkers. It was no accident that dialogue became characteristically
associated with Vatican II. Shortly before the council opened, the
young theologian Hans Urs von Balthasar published *Martin Buber
and Christianity*, in which he praised Buber as "one of the most
creative minds of our age" and "the originator of the 'dialogical
principle.'"[8]

℘

These are some of the contexts that help us understand the
council and interpret its documents. What they indicate is that new
mind-sets had taken hold in Catholicism by the time the council
opened, and they suggest that the council must be interpreted in that
light. They suggest, therefore, that in approaching the council we
should *expect* it to be different, expect it to have different views of
the Church and the world than the ones that prevailed earlier. We
should expect it not to be simply a reiteration in which nothing of
significance has changed.

Each of our authors describes other contexts that shaped
Vatican II and fills in details on the ones I sketched. They then go
on to show their relevance for getting at the meaning of the council.

Each of them, moreover, postulates that beyond the up-front issues at the council were issues under those issues, meanings beyond the grocery list of the specific provisions. The assumption that the council had a bigger message (or messages) is what makes these articles worth gathering under one cover.

The starting point for my own article is the challenge issued by Cardinal Camillo Ruini to the use of "event" as a way of describing Vatican II. Ruini used the challenge to call for a hermeneutic that will yield a "true" interpretation of the council. I try to respond to that call by outlining an approach that effectively reconciles "the letter" of the documents with "the spirit" of the council. I thus deal with an aspect of Vatican II that has been largely neglected by interpreters—the literary genre of the documents and the vocabulary that genre generates and reflects. My thesis is that this method yields an interpretation of the council that shows its special character and the significant turn the council wanted to promote in the life of the Church. That turn consisted in a new model of the Church and of its style in carrying out its mission.

The editor of *Theological Studies* asked Stephen Schloesser to write a follow-up to my article; he agreed, and his contribution appeared in the next number of the journal. Schloesser agreed with me that the council wanted to be a significant turn in the road for Catholicism; he then goes on to ask why such a turn was not only conceivable but necessary in the middle of the 20th century. To answer his question Schloesser analyzes 20th-century political and cultural shifts that framed the up-front issues at the council such as freedom of conscience and relationship with the Jews. In detail he describes new assumptions and methods that Catholic thinkers gradually appropriated in the years leading up to the council and describes the resistance those assumptions and methods often met from Catholic officials. At the council the two forces clashed, with the former winning the advantage. The two World Wars and their aftermaths are an indispensable context, according to Schloesser, for understanding this shift on the part of Catholic intellectuals and thus for understanding Vatican II. Largely as a result of the political context (with its cultural repercussions) the council wanted to project the Church as a "humanizing" force in a century that by 1962 was already the bloodiest in human history.

Neil Ormerod's article appeared just two numbers later, and it professedly wanted to build on Schloesser and me. In an opening paragraph, moreover, Ormerod acknowledges his debt to the work of Joseph Komonchek, the author of the first article in our collection. While he assesses positively Schloesser's work and mine, he sees them as essentially the work of church historians. He wants to move beyond church history to a theological analysis of the materials we two have surfaced. That is to say, he wants to move toward a historical ecclesiology. Ormerod then presents us with different models, types, and trajectories of change, drawing them from Bernard Lonergan, Robert Doran, and Christopher Dawson among others. He moves the discussion, therefore, to a closer, more theological/sociological analysis of the type of change that happened at Vatican II.

The article by Joseph Komonchak was originally a lecture delivered in 1999 at Saint Louis University. It is an analysis of three features to take into consideration in assessing the council and getting at its meaning—1) the final documents, 2) the experience of the council as reported by participants and other contemporaries, and 3) the event itself (or the council viewed as "event"). Komonchak shows how seemingly simple but actually complicated is the process of reading the documents, how fleeting was the experience of the council and how complicated the process of later trying to reconstruct it, and then shows how revealing treating the council as "event" can be. For historians an event is not merely a summary of happenings or an account of the intentions of participants but part of a larger "plot" in which the event marks a turn in the road, even a rupture. In the sense of "event," Vatican II did not end in 1965 but is still being played out in our own day. What happened *after* the council, that is to say, legitimately affects one's interpretation of what happened *during* the council.

Komonchak thus makes clear that, in studying Vatican II, we are to some extent studying ourselves and that these two studies are inseparable. In a more direct way than the other three authors, he thus reminds us of how pertinent Vatican II is to our lives today and worth our study. On one level Vatican II may be "the forgotten council," as it is sometimes described, but on another it is at work still, affecting our appreciation of what it means to be Catholic and affecting our appreciation of what the mission of the Church is for us here and now.

Notes

1. *Acta synodalia Sacrosancti Concilii Oecumenici Vaticani II*, vol. 1, part 1 (Vatican City: Typis Polyglotis Vaticani, 1970–1978) 166–75.
2. As quoted in Giuseppe Alberigo and Joseph A. Komonchak, ed., *History of Vatican II*, 5 vols. (Maryknoll, N.Y.: Orbis, 1995–2006) 1:94.
3. "Responsa ad epistolam circularem cancellarii Bismark," in *Enchiridion symbolorum*, ed. Heinrich Denzinger and Adolf Schönmetzer, 33rd ed. (New York: Herder, 1965) 603–7, at 607.
4. Pius X, "Pascendi dominici gregis," in *The Papal Encyclicals*, ed. Claudia Carlen, 5 vols. (Wilmington, N.C: McGrath, 1981) 3:71–98.
5. Henri de Lubac, *Catholicism: Christ and the Common Destiny of Man*, trans. Lancelot C. Sheppard and Elizabeth Englund (San Francisco: Ignatius, 1988) 35; original French, *Catholicisme: Les aspects sociaux du dogme* (Paris: Cerf, 1947).
6. Martin Buber, "What Is Man?" in *Between Man and Man*, trans. Ronald Gregor Smith (London: Routledge & Kegan Paul, 1947) 118–208, at 129. For an extended treatment of Buber in relation to Vatican II, see Ann Michele Nolan, *A Privileged Moment: Dialogue in the Language of the Second Vatican Council, 1962–1965* (Bern: Peter Lang, 2006) 156–76.
7. Martin Buber, "Dialogue," in *Between Man and Man* 1–39, at 7.
8. Hans Urs von Balthasar, *Martin Buber and Christianity: A Dialogue between Israel and the Church*, trans. Alexander Dru (New York: Macmillan, 1961) 9.

1.

VATICAN II
AS AN "EVENT"[1]

Joseph A. Komonchak

 The lived experience of Vatican II was in part a dramatic struggle over varying ideas about what the council ought to be, do, and say. This struggle did not end with the council. It continues today.

ON MAY 29, 1969, only three and a half years after the close of the Second Vatican Council, Henri de Lubac gave a lecture at Saint Louis University as part of the closing ceremonies celebrating the University's 150th anniversary.[2] The title of his speech as published in *Theology Digest* was "The Crisis in the Church"—a topic, he explained in the expanded French version, "suggested to him by the academic authorities" who had invited him. I refer to this lecture not only because Henri de Lubac's name honors the series in which you have kindly invited me to speak, but also because it was the fullest statement of the great French theologian's concern about what was happening in the Catholic Church in the years after the council,[3] at which, of course, he had played an important role. That something dramatic was happening in the Catholic Church was certainly clear enough by then. Two other heroes of the French theological revival also published books around the same time with significant titles: *The Decomposition of Catholicism* by Louis Bouyer and *Au milieu des orages* ("Amid the Storms") by Yves Congar.

When published both in the *Nouvelle revue théologique* and then in expanded book form, de Lubac's title was changed to *L'Église dans la crise actuelle* ("The Church in the Present Crisis"). The change clarifies one of his intentions, which was to present the troubles of the postconciliar era in light of the general crisis of the late 1960s. De Lubac was speaking only a year after the May 1968 disturbances, which had thrown the university life of France into disarray and had come close to bringing down the de Gaulle government. Americans will remember the chaos on our own campuses, the assassinations of Martin Luther King and Robert F. Kennedy, and the drama of the two political conventions that same year. "We are witnessing," de Lubac wrote, "a crisis of civilization." Relying on Erik Weil and Paul Ricoeur, de Lubac saw the crisis as a reaction to the reduction of reason to a means-focused calculation that ignores questions about meaningful ends and so has provoked, "as an alternative to the unpleasant reality of *dehumanization* and *reification*, the abstract dream of pure unregulated existence" (Weil), "the radical protest of the beatnik or the absurdity of a purposeless crime" (Ricoeur), a "universal confrontation" (de Lubac).

It was not surprising, de Lubac argued, that this crisis had evoked sympathy among some Christians, who could be expected to react against so dehumanizing a system. What was surprising was that "this same crisis has resounded with such great force even within the Church and against the Church"; the oddity was that even while fascinated by the world that was being so strongly contested, Christians were turning that same spirit of confrontation against the community of faith. "A bitter and vindictive disposition," sparing nothing, was being directed against the Church's past and present, indiscriminately attacking its structures of authority, neglecting all the positive things it had accomplished over the centuries, odiously misrepresenting its history, turning its tradition from "a living actualizing force" into "the waste-products of a dead past," regarding its authority as alien and tyrannical, the statements of its magisterium as abusive, the subjects of bitter debate, rejection, even public opposition. "I am amazed," he concluded his description, "at the good conscience of so many of the church's children who, without ever having done anything great themselves, without having thought

How true! even today.

or suffered, without taking the time to reflect, each day make themselves, to the applause of the crowds outside, the accusers of their
Mother and their brethren. . . . The whole future of the Church," de
Lubac insisted, "all the fruitfulness of its mission, all that it can and
should bring to the world, depends today on an energetic revival of
the faith. To liberate the Christian consciousness from a morbid
negativism, from a depression that is corroding it, from an inferiority
complex that is paralyzing it, from a web of ambiguities that is stifling
it, is the first condition for the renewal the Church desires."[4]

Such a renewal, of course, had been the intention of the Second
Vatican Council, and everyone appeals to it, de Lubac said, but in
different ways. "In fact," he wrote, "it is little known, little followed.
Many who claim to be the only ones to take [the council] seriously
sneer at it today. From the very beginning, a distorting interpretation
of it began to spread. Those who participated closely in it know
this."[5]

He then illustrated the point by referring in particular to the
council's Constitutions on Divine Revelation, on the Church, and
on the Church in the Modern World.

De Lubac knew that by such remarks he risked being called "a
'conservative' or 'reactionary' or 'integrist' or simply 'out of date'";
and, indeed, "fearful" and "reactionary" are words recently used to
describe his view of the postconciliar period.[6] This characterization
shows that the debate within the Church about the meaning and
validity of the Second Vatican Council continues, carried on today
both in publications and in various Web sites on the Internet. I wish
to speak today about some of the issues involved in interpreting and
evaluating the council, particularly with respect to the role that critical history might play. My intention is less that of offering my own
assessment than of suggesting some of the methodological issues
involved.

What Do We Mean by "Vatican II"?

I will begin with the three terms that defined the program of a
symposium on the council that was held in Bologna in December

1996: event, experience, and final documents.[7] The last two are the easiest to understand. "Experience" refers to contemporary intentions, motives, encounters, decisions, and actions during the council; the "final documents" are the product of that experience. The two terms differ, of course, in that while the final documents survive in the black marks on white paper, the experience is now part of the past and has to be reconstructed by the patient, critical work of historians. As important as this reconstruction may be for the interpretation of the final documents, the latter have an objectivity and continued existence that is not contained in the experience, which no longer exists except in the threatened form of ever fewer and ever fainter personal memories.

"Event" I take to represent a different category; I mean it not in the sense of a simple occurrence but in the sense of a "noteworthy" occurrence, one that has consequences. After a period in which *l'histoire événementielle* (event-centered history) appeared to have been banished in favor of the study of *la longue durée* (the longer cycle), there is now visible among the works of historians a "return of the event," "a revival of narrative," as the titles of two famous essays suggest.[8] These have been accompanied by an impressive body of historiographical literature, as reflected in two recent symposia on the meaning of the term "event."[9] The topics under discussion are varied: the relationship between continuity (structures, *mentalités*) and discontinuity (*ruptures*); the age-old question of the relations among "data," "facts," and "events"; the criteria by which to discern among historical occurrences those that qualify as "events"; the possibility of constructing a typology of "events"; the relation between contemporaries' experience, interpretation, and evaluation of historical moments and the historian's judgments about their character as "events," which raises in a different form the question of the "objectivity" of historical reconstruction; and the issue raised by Pierre Nora and others: the ability of the media to shape or even to "create" events.

In almost all of the literature, the assumption is that an "event" represents novelty, discontinuity, a "rupture," a break from routine, causing surprise, disturbance, even trauma, and perhaps initiating a new routine, a new realm of the taken-for-granted. In Pierre

Grégoire's words, an event is "a dynamic phenomenon or situation which varies enough in space and time to be perceived or undergone by the individuals involved. Consequently, for an event to be identified as such, it has to be detached in one way or another from the whole set of repetitions and regularities that constitute the course of daily life."[10] "An event," says Paul Veyne, "is difference.... An event is anything that does not go without saying."[11]

As sociology once accompanied and was used to legitimate the near-abandonment of events for the sake of studying structures, mentalities, and the longer cycle, so the return of the event in historiography has been accompanied by the development in the last two decades of what is called "historical sociology." Within that movement William Sewell has begun to work out a theory of "events" that has clear affinities with the developments in historiography just summarized.[12] Sewell conceives of events as "sequences of occurrences that result in transformations of structures." Such a sequence begins with "a rupture of some kind" that "produces reinforcing ruptures in other locations"; these ruptures then "spiral into transformative historical events when a sequence of interrelated ruptures disarticulates the previous structural network, makes repair difficult, and makes a novel rearticulation possible." Sewell illustrates his theory by a consideration of how the event at the Bastille on July 14, 1789, was transformed into that permanent change known as the French Revolution.[13]

That Vatican II constituted an "event" in this sense would seem clear and hardly in need of demonstration. Even independently of what Pope John XXIII intended the council to be, the very calling of it was a surprise, a break with the normal life of the Church. The announcement was met by both hope and fear. As the council began to unfold, the same character revealed itself, particularly in the several dramatic moments of the first session: the pope's opening speech; the postponement of the election of conciliar commissions; the vote on the liturgy schema; the severe criticism of the *De fontibus* text and its removal from the conciliar agenda;[14] the appointment of the coordinating committee to review all the preparatory material and to prepare a coherent agenda. As is clear from their accounts and journals and in essays on the council during its course, contemporaries sensed that something new and unusual was happening. People spoke of a historical turning point: the end of the Counter-Reformation or of the Tridentine era, the end of the Middle Ages, the end even of the Constantinian era. (I pass over the historiographical implications of the prayer for a "new Pentecost"!) Needless to say, the media made this novelty the main part of their story; Vatican II was front-page "news."

The event-character of the council also marked the early post-conciliar period. Within five years, articles and books began to be written, some of which enthusiastically spoke of the "new Church," "the Church of the future," "a new Christendom," while others noted with displeasure what they variously called decomposition, crisis, disaster, apostasy, etc. It is now a commonplace of histories, biographies, and autobiographies to speak of the council as a watershed; 20th-century church history is now divided into two periods: preconciliar and postconciliar.

The multi-volume *History of Vatican II* now being published gives as the subtitle of its first volume: *Toward a New Era in Catholicism*.[15] At the 1996 Bologna conference and elsewhere, important papers have been given on Vatican II as an "event."[16]

But, as it turns out, opinions are not unanimous. There are, roughly speaking, three types of interpretations of the council,[17] only two of which refer to the council as an "event," a break with earlier routine. Progressives interpret it as a good thing, the long-overdue accommodation of Catholicism to the modern world; traditionalists see it as a bad thing, the capitulation of Catholicism to principles and movements it had rightly resisted for 150 years. For both, the council was a watershed event. A third interpretation, which I have called "reformist," plays down the eventful character of the council as a break or rupture with tradition. According to Cardinal Joseph Ratzinger, whose opinion is similar to de Lubac's, the elements of discontinuity have been exaggerated by people who insist on some vague notion called the "spirit of the council" while ignoring "the authentic texts of the authentic Vatican II."

This schematism of a *before* and *after* in the history of the Church, wholly unjustified by the documents of Vatican II, which do nothing but reaffirm the continuity of Catholicism, must be decidedly opposed. There is no "pre-" or "post"-conciliar Church; there is but one, unique Church that walks the path toward the Lord, ever deepening and ever better understanding the treasure of faith that he himself has entrusted to her. There are no leaps in this history, there are no fractures, and there is no break in continuity. In no wise did the Council intend to introduce a temporal dichotomy in the Church.[18]

The cardinal's perspective is largely theological and focused on the fidelity of the council's texts to the ancient and normative faith. From a different perspective, focused on the Church's attitude to the modern world but still referring principally to the conciliar texts, French historian Émile Poulat maintains that, at most, Vatican II departed from one particular tradition; what is more obvious to him, some years after the council, is the persistence of the intransigent model characteristic of modern anti-liberal Catholicism.[19] It would seem, then, that whether Vatican II really constituted an "event" is open to debate.

Differences here in no small part depend on what is meant by "Vatican II" and particularly on whether what defines it is to be found primarily in its final texts or in the experience of both the council and its aftermath. The progressives and traditionalists focus mainly on the conciliar and postconciliar experience, which the former see as liberation and the latter as capitulation. The extreme traditionalists find capitulation even in the conciliar texts themselves, which some of the progressives also criticize for falling short of the "spirit" of Vatican II because of the many compromises made in order to placate a resistant conciliar minority. The reformists, such as Ratzinger and the later de Lubac, certainly are not unaware of the dramatic changes that have taken place in the everyday life of Catholicism, but they tend to blame them on the hijacking of the council by extreme progressives, which in turn gave and gives traditionalists reasons for rejecting the council itself; and they wish to restore some equilibrium by invoking the conciliar texts as the principal criterion for defining and understanding the council. The purpose here, of course, is not primarily historical but normative. In these three views, the main focus tends to fall on the relationship between the texts the council produced and the experience of the council. Similarly, it was in part a conviction that "Vatican II" cannot be understood solely or perhaps even primarily by reference to its final texts but has to be understood also in terms of the often conflictual intentions, experiences, actions, and encounters of participants that led to the five-volume *History of Vatican II.*[20] I will argue here, however, that the question of the meaning of Vatican II cannot be resolved simply on the basis of these two terms, "texts" and "experience"—or, if you prefer, "letter" and "spirit"—but requires critical attention to the third category—Vatican II as an "event"—which is not reducible to either of the other two terms. I will make my case primarily on historiographical grounds.

The Final Documents

It would seem that the final texts of the council provide a straightforward and easily applied criterion: if you wish to know what the council was and did, look to what it actually said. Ratzinger was not wrong when he pleaded that appeals to a vague "spirit of the council" be controlled by the "letter" of its texts. "The spirit of Vatican II" is sometimes taken to mean what certain people wanted the council to say, what it would have said if not impeded by intransigent conservatives, or what it would say today about issues that have arisen since it closed.[21] The 16 texts of Vatican II represent what the participants in the council, for good or for ill, did agree to say, and they are legitimately invoked as a now fixed expression of its intentions and authoritative decisions.

It has also to be admitted that there is an ancient principle in both canonical and civil law that a text is to be interpreted first in its most obvious and literal sense. This hermeneutic finds a parallel in recent theories of art and literature that propose ignoring or at least not favoring authorial intention: the text is what counts, and the author's intention, if not utterly irrelevant, does not exhaust its meaning. One could imagine an interpretation of the conciliar texts that would proceed in accordance with either of these two hermeneutical traditions; and perhaps something of this is what is intended when we are urged to return to the "letter" of Vatican II.

The old legal theory did maintain, however, that when a genuine question about the meaning of a text arises, recourse must be had to the intention of the legislator. In our case this would mean attending to the redactional history of the conciliar texts, which, after all, did not fall ready-made from heaven. They are the result of a history that runs at least from the antepreparatory consultation, through the official preparatory texts, through the revisions made during the council, down to the final promulgation. Anyone who has worked on the final texts knows that their full meaning can often be found only when they are placed within this redactional history. What has been changed, added, eliminated in this process often provides helpful indications of what was intended in the final texts, for many of which we have also explicit testimonies from the revising bodies of what successive texts meant and of what various changes in them signified.[22] These are, it hardly needs to be said, enormously important for a hermeneutic of the texts, history now itself becoming an indispensable element in their interpretation. In many of these redactional histories, the differences between the texts officially prepared and the final texts are great enough for one to be able to speak at times of "break" or "discontinuity." This is true not only of what they said but also of the style and tone in which they said it, a point pertinently made by John O'Malley.[23]

But there is still another consideration. Many, if not all, of the more significant conciliar texts are part of a history larger than the one that began with the preparatory period or with the antepreparatory consultation, and they are larger also than a history that ends with their promulgation. Consider a historical hermeneutic of *Dei verbum*. One way to begin is with the text *De fontibus revelationis* that was prepared by the Preparatory Theological Commission. A whole set of questions will arise as soon as it is compared with the council's Dogmatic Constitution, among them: How did it happen that the council, which was expected to say what was said in

De fontibus, said finally what is said in *Dei verbum*? Where are the points of continuity, of discontinuity, etc.? But then there is the question about the *De fontibus* text itself: Why did the council treat the questions it discussed? Why did it adopt the positions it took? Answers to these questions may lead us back to the antepreparatory consultation, which in turn will open upon larger questions about recent interpretations of the Bible, ecumenical relations, etc. And these open upon a still larger history that will include the encyclical *Divino afflante Spiritu* (1943), the decrees of the Pontifical Biblical Commission, the syllabus *Lamentabili sane exitu* (1907), the encyclical *Pascendi dominici gregis* (1907), and the Modernist crisis, the rise of historical criticism, the relation between Scripture and tradition in posttridentine Catholicism, the crisis of the Reformation—behind which, of course, lies a still earlier history. But perhaps enough has been said to indicate how large the series can be made within which to make sense both of the text *De fontibus* and the conciliar text *Dei verbum*, and to warrant the conclusion that the latter text was certainly intended to do something other than simply "reaffirm the continuity of Catholicism."

The Experience of the Council

If we turn now to the other term, "experience," things are even more complex. Often used in the singular, the term would seem to refer to "what happened during Vatican II," now considered to be something larger than the simple preparation of the final documents. The term "experience," or terms like it, was used at the time of the council, as, for example, in descriptions of what happened to many bishops who found themselves meeting for the first time in their lives in and as a council.[24] Even then, however, this usage was deceptive because it reduced to a single experience, and a single experience of a certain type, what was in fact a plurality and a variety of individual experiences. It was the experience of the majority that was considered to count as "Vatican II." Most of the first accounts and histories of the council were written by the "victors."

But what now, more than 40 years later, do we mean by Vatican II as an "experience"? If we initially restrict ourselves again to the interval from January 25, 1959, to December 8, 1965, the term may refer to all that happened at the council as lived by its participants during that time frame. But two difficulties arise at this point. The first is the problem sometimes referred to by historiographers as that of "abstraction" in history. Many years ago American historian Carl Becker pointed out that Caesar's crossing of the Rubicon, apparently a simple and certain "fact" of history, in fact is "a generalization of a thousand and one simpler facts."[25] Similarly, Paul Veyne notes that the "French Revolution" is a term used to cover "an aggregate of little facts."[26] Neither of these two observations renders the use of a single covering term illegitimate, but they do urge caution upon us when we use a term like "Vatican II" and perhaps particularly when we are tempted to speak of it as having been a single "experience."

Apart from the moments at which the participants took official and collective action, it is difficult to speak of a single "experience" of the council. If this term is broken down into intentions, motives, encounters, decisions, actions, we will be struck by the diversity of experiences that may be imagined or reconstructed in the two popes, the 2,500 bishops, the thousands of experts, functionaries, observers, auditors, journalists, etc., and the hundreds or thousands of encounters that constituted the daily tissue of the council. It is probable that the majority of participants have left no traces of their contemporary "experience" of the council. Among those who did leave some trace, historical reconstruction will surely discover that what they lived and experienced varied considerably, not only because of personal backgrounds but also because of theological or ideological orientation and because of the degrees and manners of their participation. Some of them will have been major protagonists, others quite minor. Some will have been members of the "progressive" majority, others of the "conservative" minority, still others somewhere in the middle. There will have been not inconsiderable differences within these three camps. We are very far from having accomplished the very first, and merely preliminary, historical task of assembling and interpreting the materials that will give us access to their contemporary "experiences" of the council. It will be tempting, whether now at this incomplete first stage or later when it is farther advanced, to select out of all these experiences certain ones that will be considered *the* experience of the council.

On the other hand, one might anticipate that from the varied reconstructed experiences of the council there will emerge a common experience of discontinuity, in whatever way it is to be interpreted or evaluated. For example, the experiences of Cardinals Augustin Bea and Alfredo Ottaviani with regard to the fate of the *De fontibus* text one may expect to have been quite varied—the first joyful, the second disappointed. But these would be varied personal responses to a common fact: that the text prepared by Ottaviani and opposed by Bea had been removed from the conciliar agenda and remanded to a mixed commission. Similarly, the *coup d'église* that was accomplished at the first session would have been experienced differently by the "victors" and the "vanquished"; but the fact would remain that those who had controlled the preparation of the council had lost control of the council itself to those who had been largely extraneous to its preparation. In both cases, then, the first session will have been experienced as an "event," a break with routine.

Experience and the Historian's "Event"

But should a critical history of the council aim for a reconstruction of the "experience" of the council? For that reconstruction will merely attain the (partial) information about the council that was communicated in various ways by (some of) those who participated in it. This is not yet critical history, which aims at a rounded view of what was under way, a view of which few, if any, of the participants may have been fully aware. This is the critical point at which the historian's judgment cannot be limited to what even the chief and most influential protagonists intended or experienced. Thus, for example, to decide whether Vatican II was or was not an "event," that is, a rupture, it is not enough to establish that this was what Pope John XXIII and others intended or what still others resisted, nor even to establish that all or some of them experienced it as a "rupture." If their intentions in one direction or another are not irrelevant to the historian's judgment as to whether or not Vatican II was an "event," they are only a part, and perhaps not even the most important part, of what must enter into that judgment. For whether or not a rupture is taking place can be quite independent of the intentions and experiences of participants and contemporaries. Some who intend to bring about a rupture may find that no rupture has taken place; some who intend a particular type of rupture may find that quite another has taken place; some who had no intention at all of effecting a rupture may find that one has nevertheless taken place. Mikhail Gorbachev may have desired glasnost, but he does not seem to have intended the dismemberment of the Communist empire.

All this is to say that a judgment about whether or not Vatican II is an "event," a break, a rupture, a discontinuity, cannot rest solely on the experiences, intentions, motives, etc., of the participants in the council. This is a historical judgment, which means that it is a historian's judgment. History is not simply the reproduction of contemporaries' experiences; it is a judgment about what contemporaries are quite often unaware of. One might recall Veyne's general remark, "the lived reality as it comes from the hands of the historian is not that of the actors,"[27] and then apply to Vatican II his comments about the Battle of Waterloo. As a historian tells this story, it is not simply the sum total of the experiences of Napoleon, Marshal Ney, ordinary soldiers, or canteen workers. Rather, "it is a choice, and a critical choice, of what witnesses saw. . . . From the testimonies and documents the historian cuts out the event he has chosen to produce; that is why an event never coincides with the cogito of its actors and witnesses."[28]

The same is true of that "aggregate of little facts" called "Vatican II." What a historian calls that event does not simply coincide with the intentions of John XXIII, of Paul VI, of Cardinal Ottaviani, of Cardinal Bea, of Cardinal Suenens, of Cardinal Lercaro, of Archbishop Lefebvre, of Bishop Wojtyla, or of any or all of the other protagonists who have left various documents that are the traces through which for now the council is principally mediated and which soon will be the only means by which the historian has access to it. To investigate and publish their testimonies will provide an indispensable mine of information for the historian who wishes to describe the "event" of Vatican II; but his description, in the form of a narrative of the council, will not coincide with any one of these testimonies and will be something other than the simple sum total of such testimonies, if such a thing can even be imagined. It is likely that the story that the historian will quite legitimately desire to tell is one of which none of them was aware. History often tells what contemporaries did not know or consciously "live."

"Event" as Episode in a Plot

There is another consideration that must be taken into account if one believes that one can apply to Vatican II the general observation made by Veyne: "An event has meaning only within a series," to which he immediately adds, "the number of series is indefinite."[29] Becker illustrates the point with Caesar's crossing of the Rubicon:

> It can't mean anything except as it is absorbed into the complex web of circumstances which brought it into being. . . . Apart from these great events and complicated relations, the crossing of the Rubicon means nothing, is not a historical fact properly speaking at all. In itself it is nothing for us; it becomes something for us, not in itself, but as a symbol of something else, a symbol standing for a long series of events which have to do with the most intangible and immaterial realities, viz.: the relation between Caesar and the millions of people of the Roman world.[30]

This means, in turn, that an event makes sense only within a story. Here again Veyne makes the point crisply: "Since it has a meaning, an event, whatever it is, implies a context; it refers to a plot of which it is an episode."[31] The story one wishes to tell and the plot one assigns it determine what will count as an "event" and what will not. Change the story and the plot line, and some incidents suddenly become important while others recede into insignificance. This I take to be simply another way of expressing the fact that the historian does not begin by establishing the brute "facts" and then looking for their interconnections. There are no brute "facts" in this sense; there are only "traces," "data," that do not "speak" on their own but are elevated to the status of "evidence" only when a historian approaches them with a question, a hypothesis, a potential story to tell.[32] This is the essential and valid point made long ago by Lucien Febvre when he spoke of the historian as one "to whom Providence has supplied no brute facts, facts extraordinarily endowed with a perfectly defined, simple, irreducible existence. It is the historian who calls into existence even the humblest of historical facts."[33]

And elsewhere: "To work out a fact is to construct. If you will, it is to supply an answer to a question. And if there is no question, there is only nothing."[34] It is only the lingering legacy of positivism that still arouses fears that this introduces the Trojan horse of "subjectivity" into the pursuit of an "objective" history or that makes some people conclude that relativism is inescapable in history.[35] Neither position admits that authentic subjectivity might transcend itself in objectivity.

What are some implications of these observations? A first is the crucial significance of the timeline chosen for the history of any event, since any story, any narrative, must have a beginning, a middle, and an end. In the case of Vatican II, almost everyone today, from contemporary journalists to critical historians, takes it for granted that the story line within which the council is an episode begins before the council. The disagreement arises over how far back to extend that timeline, a judgment that may depend on the nature and content of the story one wishes to tell. Different timelines may be appropriate for different conciliar documents: how far back must one go, for example, to render intelligible the issuing of *Dignitatis humanae* or of *Dei verbum*?

But the perhaps more interesting question is whether the timeline, and so the story within which one tries to make sense of Vatican II, should be considered to end on December 8, 1965. For surely in the plot of any story, the final scene is as important as the first, and perhaps even more important because in any drama it is the last act that makes plain the meaning of the earlier acts. Perhaps I may borrow from Hayden White and Keith Jenkins the following argument.[36] Imagine a series of chronologically sequential facts or incidents—a b c d e . . . n—about which one wishes to construct a narrative that will go beyond mere chronology. The incidents may be arranged in one of the following manners:

1. **A** b c d c . . . n
2. a **B** c d e . . . n
3. a b **C** d e . . . n
4. a b c **D** e . . . n
5. a b c d **E** . . . n

In each of the five possibilities, the letter capitalized in bold print indicates that a certain incident is being given privileged dramatic status. Stressing one of these incidents establishes relationships among them all; it elevates the incident chosen from its mere place in the chronological sequence and gives it some sort of explanatory role vis-à-vis the others: if "A" is chosen, the explanation is likely to be causal; if "E" is chosen, the explanation is likely to be teleological. More than that, this choice may also determine which of the other sequential incidents deserves notice at all, because some of them are "incidental" to the plot of the story being told and may reasonably and responsibly be left out.

When Does the Story End?

Apply this scheme now to Vatican II. Does Vatican II appear at the end of one's story, or does the story continue? If one's story ends with Vatican II, one will certainly be tempted in the direction of a "Whig" interpretation, seeing the council as the telos of one's plot. But even apart from that temptation, often indulged, there is the simple fact that the history of the Church, the larger series within which Vatican II is an episode, did not end with the close of the council. Is "Vatican II" the same "event," then, in 2007 as it was thought to be in 1965? (I have heard it claimed that "history" one day will regard the pontificate of John Paul II as more significant—more "eventful"—than the Second Vatican Council.) It is not enough to say that one wishes to tell only this one part of the larger story, the one that includes only that "aggregate of little facts" that occurred between 1959 and 1965. Here is where the primary importance of one's story and its plot becomes clear. All those "simpler facts" are facts only within the story one chooses to tell, and the story, and where and how it ends, will determine which of them receive one's attention and find a place in the final narrative. Facts that are part of one story will not enter into another.

The fact is that it is only by abstraction that the phenomenon studied as "Vatican II" can be considered to have ended with its final solemn session. The passion often displayed in competing interpretations of the council today is very often a function of what happened after the council, with the question of whether it happened *because of* the council being a major point at issue. And in the case of both Ratzinger and Poulat, the judgment that Vatican II should not be considered an "event" in the sense of a "rupture" rests very much on their assessments of what happened after and even of what is happening today. Most historians today in fact approach the council with an awareness of what happened after it closed. Nor should this be considered inappropriate. Bernard Lonergan puts the point well:

> It is the occurrence of later events that place earlier events in a new perspective. The outcome of a battle fixes the perspective in which the successive stages of the battle are viewed; military victory in a war reveals the significance of the successive battles that were fought; the social and cultural consequences of the victory and the defeat are the measure of the effects of the war. So, in general, history is an ongoing process. As the process advances, the context within which events are to be understood keeps enlarging. As the context enlarges, perspectives shift.[37]

I wish to insist that this does not mean simply that one might decide also to write the history of the "reception" of Vatican II as a later project covering the time span of the decades since it closed.

It also means that what happened *after* the council legitimately influences one's study of what happened *during* the council. What Lonergan calls the new "perspective" enabled by the "enlarged context" yields new questions for the sake of a different story. That new perspective enables one to notice things one might not have noticed before, to drop things an earlier perspective had highlighted, to assign different weight to the same things, to see interconnections not suspected before, etc. Febvre's comment remains pertinent: it is easy enough to describe what you see; seeing what ought to be described is the hard part. Without the questions enabled by a perspective, there is nothing.

These remarks are pertinent not only to a discussion of the "event" character of Vatican II on a grand scale but also to the other two elements in our discussion: the final documents and the experience. Take the example, already used, of *Dei verbum*. A critical history of this text will certainly place it within a series that began long before the council was imagined. May it not also be affected by what happened after the council closed? I mean here not only a discussion of its "reception," what influence it has had on Catholic attitudes and habits with regard to the Scriptures, how it has affected an understanding of the magisterium, what impact it has had on ecumenical treatments of the relation between Scripture and tradition, etc. I mean also, for example, the current status of biblical hermeneutics, which are in a rather different state than they were at the time of the council. Different questions are being asked about the relation between historical-critical methods and the use of the Bible in the liturgy and catechesis, or about interpretations of the Bible that may presuppose historical-critical conclusions but, refusing to be limited to them, explore various other, more literary, theological, and spiritual readings—some of which are not unlike the way in which the fathers and monastic theologians approached and applied the Scriptures.

The history of Catholic biblical interpretation, in other words, does not end with the promulgation of *Dei verbum*, and when this further history is taken into account, one's understanding of what was under way in this regard at Vatican II is altered, precisely because the story continues. Now one might notice what is otherwise unnoticed: that the two camps into which the protagonists of the history of *Dei verbum* are often divided may have had more in common than appeared. Both of them placed primary emphasis on the literal sense: one may have understood it as a set of proof texts for theological arguments, the other as what emerges when one places them and their authors in historical context. Alien to both camps was a type of exegesis that sought to validate the spiritual and typological interpretations of Scripture that prevailed in the patristic and early medieval eras and in the use of the Bible in the liturgy. Vatican II vindicated the historical-critical approach against the suspicions of the dogmatists—a fact most often pointed to as the real achievement of *Dei verbum*, particularly when its history is thought to end with its promulgation. But the recent developments in biblical hermeneutics remind one of another part of the history of 20th-century Catholic interpretations of the Bible, and this postconciliar development raises questions about a dimension largely neglected in commentaries on *Dei verbum*, its last chapter, on the use of the Bible in the Church. In this larger history, what "Vatican II" said or did not say has different dimensions; a different story and plot suggest attention to other incidents, positions, and protagonists both at and before the council.

The example illustrates that even the apparently straightforward history of the redaction of conciliar texts is more complex than is often thought, and that the historian's determination of a timeline for this history is of crucial significance. It is likely that similar remarks could be made about almost all of the council's final documents, which are "final" only on one timeline and within only one of many possible plots.

Similar remarks can be made about what is called the "experience" of the council. Part of this was what I earlier called the *coup d'église*, whereby bishops and theologians who were at best marginal and at worst under active suspicion by Roman authority became the leaders of the conciliar event as it worked out. Toward the end of the council, cracks began to appear within the phalanx of "progressive" theologians (as they were known at the time), and within five years or so of its close, these cracks had widened into open breaks, of which the two journals, *Concilium* and *Communio*, may be taken as symbolic. Differences in the interpretation of Vatican II played no small part in this breach, not to mention differences in the evaluation of what happened afterward and in judgments about its relation to the council.

The appearance of this division within the "progressive" ranks provides another new perspective on what was happening during Vatican II, yielding new questions and new hypotheses, for the sake of a fuller story. For one thing, it calls into question the adequacy of the common division of the conciliar protagonists into "progressives" and "conservatives" and therefore complicates the plot of the conciliar drama itself. One becomes more alert to the differences between, say, a Congar or Chenu and a Daniélou or de Lubac, or between a Rahner and a Ratzinger; and attention to such differences may yield new questions about a Dossetti and a Küng. One begins to read the writings of these men more closely and carefully; one becomes more alert to differences in theological methodology and in conciliar tactics. Dimensions of the contemporary "experience" of the council that might have escaped one's attention beforehand are now noticed and may be reconstructed.

Another example can be found in a recent book on the women auditors at Vatican II.[38] The research behind the book was prompted by two postconciliar phenomena: the influence of feminism on the Church and what the author interprets as the present pope's efforts to subvert Vatican II. Though insufficiently critical and comprehensive, the book has the merit of drawing attention to the activities of those women, including their participation in drafting conciliar texts, which have received less attention than they appear to deserve: a neglected dimension of the conciliar "experience." Other examples might be simply noted: since the council, the flourishing of the theology of the local church directs attention and prompts new questions about the ecclesiological disputes at the council; the rise of the churches of the southern hemisphere raises issues easily overlooked when the largely "North Atlantic" set of concerns is taken to define the conciliar "experience"; the dispute about whether the council should be "doctrinal" or "pastoral" appears more complex when postconciliar interest in "inculturation" is part of one's horizon; the spread of what is called "postmodernity" gives new dimensions to the familiar interpretation of the council in terms of a new confrontation between Catholicism and "modernity."

I am not here proposing anachronistic impositions of postconciliar problematics upon the council itself. I am simply asking that historians of Vatican II be aware that to make the council the last scene in one's story is to tell only one of many possible stories, even of what happened between 1959 and 1965, and that what was under way then will be told differently if one's plot does not make the council the last scene in the drama.[39] This recognition is all the more important if, as is the case, all reflection on the council, even the most rigorously critical, takes place today in an ecclesial and cultural context in which the interpretation and evaluation of what happened after, and surely in part and at least in some senses *because of* the council, is a major and divisive factor. Not to recognize this and not to acknowledge it explicitly is to raise questions about the properly critical character of one's history.

This brings me to my last point. It is reasonably clear to everyone that the inner dynamic of the council, the lived "experience," was in part that of a dramatic struggle between or among varying ideas about what Vatican II ought to be, to do, and to say. It is just as clear that this struggle did not end with the council, and that the question of how the Church ought to be at once faithful to Christ and an effective sign and instrument of him in the world or worlds of today continues. It is only natural that disagreements about these matters will affect one's initial interest in the council, the questions one asks, the elements one assembles in order to answer them, the story one decides to tell, and, above all, one's *evaluation of* the conciliar event. I do not believe that there is any way in which these larger issues can be wiped from a historian's mind, nor do I think that anything but a purely mythical ideal of "presuppositionless history" should require one to try to do so. But I do think that it might help if we were to acknowledge that the last thing to which I referred above—the evaluation of the council—represents a different level of the historian's existential involvement in his project and that gross differences on this level will not be resolved by the same criteria by which the historian attempts to say "what really happened at Vatican II." It is too much to expect that mere history will suffice to overcome those differences, which have other causes and require other solutions.

Notes

1. The article first appeared in *Theology Digest* 46 (Winter 1999) 337–52, as the published version of the fourth annual Henri de Lubac Lecture in Historical Theology, delivered at Saint Louis University on February 11, 1999. The current version contains minor changes to bring the article up to date. It retains the lecture format, but as if it were being delivered in 2007.
2. Henri de Lubac, "The Church in Crisis," *Theology Digest* 17 (1969) 312–25. The lecture, delivered May 29, 1969, was also published in *Nouvelle revue théologique* 91 (1969) 580–96 and then expanded into a 97-page booklet, *L'Église dans la crise actuelle* (Paris: Cerf, 1969). The English text misses some of the nuance of the French version.
3. The argument had been anticipated two years earlier in de Lubac's presentation at the Congress on the Theology of the Renewal of the Church, Toronto, August 1967; see Henri de Lubac, S.J., "Teilhard de Chardin in the Context of Renewal," in *Theology of Renewal*, vol. 1, *Renewal of Religious Thought*, ed. L. K. Shook (New York: Herder & Herder, 1968) 208–35, esp. 212–17.
4. Henri de Lubac, "L'Église dans la crise actuelle," *Nouvelle revue théologique* 91 (1969) 580–96, at 582–83, 586
5. Ibid. 587.
6. See *The HarperCollins Encyclopedia of Catholicism*, ed. Richard P. McBrien (San Francisco: Harper, 1995) 797.
7. All three terms appeared in the official program of the meeting, but only two of them appear in the title of the volume in which the major papers delivered at this meeting have been published: *L'evento e le decisioni: Studi sulle dinamiche del concilio Vaticano II*, ed. Maria Teresa Fattori and Alberto Melloni (Bologna: Il Mulino, 1997). The omission of "experience" from the title of the published volume reflects the apparent failure of my

presentation there (of which this paper is an altered version) to convince others that the "event" of the council is not reducible to the "experience" of the council.

8. See Pierre Nora, "Le retour de l'événement" in *Faire de l'histoire* (Paris: Gaillimard, 1974) vol. 1: 210–28; Lawrence Stone, "The Revival of Narrative: Reflections on a New Old History," *Past and Present* 85 (1979) 3–24. For the French debate, see Peter Burke, *The French Historical Revolution: The* Annales *School 1929–1989* (Stanford, Calif.: Stanford University, 1990); Mauro Moretti, "Fragments d'une analyse historiographique: Origines et premiers développements d'un 'discours sur l'événement' dans l'expérience des 'Annales,'" in *L'événement: Actes du Colloque organisé a Aix-en-Provence par le Centre Méridional d'Histoire Sociale, les 16, 17, et 18 septembre 1983* (Aix-en-Provence: Université de Provence, 1986) 182–202; and Jacques Revel, "Introduction," in *Histories: French Constructions of the Past* (New York: New Press, 1995) 1–63. For the wider discussion, see Richard J. Evans, *In Defense of History* (New York: Norton, 1998).

9. See *L'événement* (cited in the previous note) and Claire Dolan, ed., *Événement, identité, et histoire* (Sillery, Quebec: Septentrion 1991).

10. Pierre Grégoire, "L'événement-référence: Notion d'évenément et plans de références: L'individu, les systemes d'information, et l'histoire-mémoire," in *Evénément, identité, et histoire* 171.

11. Paul Veyne, *Comment on écrit l'histoire* (Paris: Seuil, 1978) 18.

12. William H. Sewell, Jr., "A Theory of Structure: Duality, Agency, and Social Transformation," *American Journal of Sociology* 98 (1992) 1–29; Sewell, "Three Temporalities: Toward an Eventful Sociology," in *The Historic Turn in the Human Sciences*, ed. Terrence McDonald (Ann Arbor: University of Michigan, 1996) 245–80; "Historical Events as Transformations of Structures: Inventing Revolution at the Bastille," *Theory and Society* 25 (1996) 841–81.

13. Andrew Greeley drew on Sewell's theory and this illustration to argue that Vatican II represents another example of an "event":

"The Revolutionary Event of Vatican II: How Everything Changed," *Commonweal* 125.15 (1998) 14–20.

14. A text on the sources of revelation, prepared by the Theological Commission, was harshly criticized by some important prelates. When 61 percent of the bishops voted to end discussion of the draft, Pope John XXIII ordered it remanded to a mixed commission for review and revision.

15. At the time of this lecture, only volumes 1 to 3 had appeared. The entire five-volume study was completed in May 2006. See Giuseppe Alberigo and Joseph A. Komonchak, eds., *History of Vatican II*, 5 vols. (Maryknoll, N.Y.: Orbis, 1995–2006).

16. See Etienne Fouilloux, "Histoire et événement: Vatican II," *Cristianesimo nella storia* 13 (1992) 515–38; Fouilloux, "La categoria di evento nella storiografia francese recente"; Peter Hünermann, "Il concilio Vaticano II come evento"; and Joseph A. Komonchak, "Riflessioni storiografiche sul Vaticano II come evento," all in *L'evento e le dicisioni*, respectively pp. 52–62, 63–92, and 417–39; Claude Soetens, "Le Concile comme événement: Une prise de conscience progressive," in *Vatican II et la Belgique*, ed. Claude Soetens (Ottignies: Quorum, 1996) 83–113.

17. See Fouilloux, "Histoire et événement," whose typology roughly coincides with the one I offer in "Interpreting the Second Vatican Council," *Landas* 1 [aratic] (1987) 81–90, and in "Interpreting the Council: Catholic Attitudes toward Vatican II," in *Being Right: Conservative Catholics in America*, ed. Mary Jo Weaver and R. Scott Appleby (Bloomington: Indiana University, 1995) 17–36.

18. Joseph Ratzinger with Vittorio Messori, *The Ratzinger Report: An Exclusive Interview on the State of the Church* (San Francisco: Ignatius, 1985) 27–44, at 35.

19. Émile Poulat, *Une Église ébranlée: Changement, conflit, et continuité de Pie XII à Jean-Paul II* (Tournai-Paris: Casterman, 1980) 288–99.

20. See the essay by the project's director, Giuseppe Alberigo, "Luci e ombre nel rapporto tra dinamica assembleare e conclusioni conciliari," in *L'evento e le decisioni* 501–22.

21. I am reminded of Bernard Lonergan's quip about doctoral dissertations that judged much later thinkers by comparison with "the principles of the Angelic Doctor": "This is what St. Thomas Aquinas would have said to, say, John Dewey, if St. Thomas Aquinas were the author of the dissertation."

22. An illustrative case is the meaning of the phrase "*subsistit in*" in *Lumen gentium* no. 8. One may interpret it simply as it stands and add a dose of philosophy with a result such as that of the Congregation for the Doctrine of the Faith: "The Council instead chose the word 'subsists' precisely to make clear that there exists only one 'subsistence' of the true Church, that outside its visible structure exist only 'elements of the Church,' which—being elements of the same Church—tend and lead toward the Catholic Church" (Congregation for the Doctrine of the Faith, *Documenta inde a Concilio Vaticano Secundo expleto edita [1966–1985]* [Rome: Libreria Editrice Vaticana, 1985] 288). But there is no indication that speculations about "subsistence" played any role whatever in the decision to replace the simple "*est*" of the previous version of this text with "*subsistit in,*" and the Doctrinal Commission's explanation of the change is much simpler.

23. See John W. O'Malley, *Tradition and Transition: Historical Perspectives on Vatican II* (Wilmington, Del.: Michael Glazier, 1989).

24. Two examples may be cited from the young Joseph Ratzinger's *Theological Highlights of Vatican II* (New York: Paulist, 1966), comments written after each of the council's four sessions. Referring to the debate on the *De fontibus* text at the first session, he wrote, "But everything that had happened since the Council began had basically changed the situation. The bishops were no longer the same men they had been before the Council" (21). Commenting on the debates at the third session, he noted that "in the common struggle for truth, statements were boldly made which five years ago would have been virtually unthinkable. . . . This spiritual awakening, which the bishops accomplished in full view of the Church, or, rather, accomplished *as* the Church, was the great and irrevocable event of the Council. It was more important in many respects than the texts it passed, for these

texts could only voice a part of the new life which had been awakened in this encounter of the Church with its inner self" (132).

25. Carl L. Becker, *Detachment and the Writing of History: Essays and Letters of Carl L. Becker*, ed. Phil L. Snyder (Ithaca, N.Y.: Cornell University, 1958) 43–45.

26. Veyne, *Comment on écrit l'histoire* 131 n.

27. Ibid. 18.

28. Ibid. 61–62; see also p. 15: "Even if I am a contemporary and witness of Waterloo, even if I am the principal actor, or Napoleon himself, I will have only one perspective on what the historians will call the event of Waterloo; all I can do is leave posterity my testimony, which, if it survives, posterity will call a trace." See the similar remarks of Bernard Lonergan: "In military terms, history is concerned, not just with the opposing commanders' plans of the battle, not just with the experiences of the battle had by each soldier and officer, but with the actual course of the battle as the resultant of conflicting plans now successfully and now unsuccessfully executed. In brief, where exegesis is concerned to determine what a particular person meant, history is concerned to determine what, in most cases, contemporaries do not know" (Bernard J. F. Lonergan, *Method in Theology* [New York: Herder & Herder, 1972] 179). See also Henri Irénée. Marrou, *De la connaissance historique* (Paris: Seuil, 1962) 47, commenting on the incomplete knowledge possessed by contemporaries: "The historian cannot be content with such a view, so fragmentary and superficial; he wants and seeks to know about it much more than any contemporaries of the time knew about it or could have known about it."

29. Veyne, *Comment on écrit l'histoire* 41.

30. Becker, *Detachment and the Writing of History* 44–45.

31. Veyne, *Comment on écrit l'histoire* 53.

32. "Historians' questions turn the material remains from the past into evidence, for evidence is only evidence in relation to a particular account" (Joyce Appleby, Lynn Hunt, and Margaret Jacob, *Telling the Truth about History* [New York: Norton, 1995] 261).

33. Lucien Febvre, *Combats pour l'histoire* (Paris: Armand Colin, 1992) 23. This is not a problem confined to historians but occurs also in the physical sciences. Febvre several times refers to his own experience of looking through a scientist-friend's microscope and being unable to see anything: "to describe what one sees—that's easy; to see what ought to be described—that's what's difficult" (8, 22–23, 431).

34. Ibid. 8; see also 7, where Febvre evokes the positivist's horror at the thought that history involves choice: "'The historian doesn't choose facts. Choose? By what right? On what principle? Choice is the denial of scientific work.'" To which Febvre replies: "But all history is choice." It is not irreverent to point to the original conclusion of the Fourth Gospel, which in the main surely applies also to the Synoptics: "Jesus did many other signs in the presence of the disciples, which are not written in this book; but these are written that you may believe that Jesus is the Christ, the Son of God" (Jn 20:30–31).

35. "Despite this generation's scorn for positivism, positivism has left as its principal legacy an enduring dichotomy between absolute objectivity and totally arbitrary interpretations of the world of objects" (Appleby et al., *Telling the Truth about History* 246). For those historiographers known in the anglophone world as "metahistorians," because the past was not lived consciously as the story that the historian tells, any correspondence-theory of truth is irrelevant, and one must conclude with Keith Jenkins that "all history is interpretive and never literally true (besides anything else, a 'true interpretation' is an oxymoron)" (Keith Jenkins, *On 'What Is History?': From Carr and Elton to Rorty and White* [New York: Routledge, 1995] 23). For the general question see also Peter Novick, *That Noble Dream: The "Objectivity Question" and the American Historical Profession* (New York: Cambridge University, 1988), esp. part 4, "Objectivity in Crisis" 415–629.

36. Jenkins (*On 'What Is History?'* 152), who refers to Hayden White, *Tropics of Discourse: Essays in Cultural Criticism* (Baltimore: Johns Hopkins, 1978) 92–93.

37. Lonergan, *Method in Theology* 192. Compare Marrou, *De la connaissance historique* 46: "But this interval that separates us from the past object is not an empty space; in the intervening time the events studied—whether they are actions, thoughts, feelings—have borne their fruit, entailed consequences, unfolded their potentialities, and we cannot separate our knowledge of those events from our knowledge of their sequels." Mao Tse-tung (or was it Chou En-lai?), when asked what he thought of the French Revolution, is said to have replied: "It's too soon to tell."

38. Carmel McEnroy, *Guests in Their Own House: The Women of Vatican II* (New York: Crossroad, 1996).

39. See Marrou, *De la connaissance historique* 46–47: "The very effort that led me to conclude that Jansenism is a bastard development of Augustinianism greatly helped me to a better understanding of the latter."

2.

VATICAN II: DID ANYTHING HAPPEN?

John W. O'Malley, S.J.

Recent emphasis on the continuity of Vatican II with the Catholic tradition runs the danger of slighting the aspects of the council that were discontinuous. Among those aspects are the literary genre the council adopted and the vocabulary inherent in the genre, different from that of all previous councils. Examination of these aspects yields tools for constructing a hermeneutic appropriate to this *council, and not only shows how distinctive Vatican II was but also allows us to get at that elusive "spirit of the council." The substance of this article was delivered as the Roland Bainton Lecture for 2005 at the Divinity School of Yale University and shortly afterwards as one of the "Gathering Points" lectures at Marquette University.*

ON JUNE 17, 2005, in the Pietro da Cortona room of the Capitoline Museums in Rome, Cardinal Camillo Ruini, the pope's vicar for the diocese of Rome and president of the Italian Bishops' Conference, made a public presentation of a new book by Archbishop Agostino Marchetto and published by the Vatican Press, *The Ecumenical Council Vatican II: A Counterpoint for Its History.*[1] Such "presentations" for new publications are not unusual in Italy, but this one was special because of the official and, indeed, eminent status of the presenter, because of the elegant, public, and civic venue of the presentation, because of its attack on other scholars, and because of the coverage the presentation therefore received even in the secular press.[2]

Ruini welcomed the new book because, according to him, it acts as a counterpoint, indeed as the polar opposite of the interpretation of Vatican II that until now has monopolized the historiography of the council. He sees Marchetto as moving us along the road to a "correct" understanding. But Ruini, in line with Marchetto, did not let the matter rest there. He singled out "the Bologna School," whose *capo* is Professor Giuseppe Alberigo, as the principal and most influential creator of the incorrect understanding.

More specifically he attacked the *magnum opus* of the Bologna-based Institute for Religious Sciences: the recently completed, multi-authored, five-volume history of the council edited by Alberigo and published almost simultaneously in six languages—Italian, French, German, Spanish, Portuguese, and English.[3] Ruini, like Marchetto, compared the Alberigo volumes to the history of the Council of Trent written by Paolo Sarpi, which was published in London in 1619 and immediately placed on the Index of Forbidden Books.[4] Sarpi's thesis, baldly put: Trent was a papal conspiracy to prevent the reform of the Church. A more damning comparison could hardly be imagined.

What, in the Ruini/Marchetto view, is wrong with Alberigo's approach? Many things, among which are: an anticurial bias, comparisons of Pope Paul VI with John XXIII unfavorable to the former, emphasis on the so-called novelty of the council and its differences from previous councils, an underlying "reformist" ideology, and, finally, diminishing the importance of the official final documents of the council in favor of the council as "event."

These criticisms are all interrelated, but the sticking point is the last, for by describing the council as "event"[5] Alberigo has borrowed a term and idea from secular social scientists that means a rupture, a change from received norms and ways, a "before" and an "after." The documents of the council do nothing, according to Ruini and Marchetto, but insist on their continuity with the Catholic tradition. Alberigo presents the council as a "new beginning" in the history of the Church, which Ruini dismisses as "theologically inadmissible." He goes on to say: "The interpretation of the council as a rupture and a new beginning is coming to an end. This interpretation is very feeble today and has no real foothold in the body of the Church. It is time for historiography to produce a new reconstruction of Vatican II that will also be, finally, a true story."[6] What is needed, according to Ruini and Marchetto, is a new hermeneutic that will reveal the true nature of the council.

Ruini sometimes seems almost to be paraphrasing Cardinal Joseph Ratzinger, who in 1985 similarly insisted on no "before" and no "after" the council.[7] In any case, the Ruini/Marchetto incident is not an altogether isolated phenomenon. Other publications have recently been following the same almost-exclusive emphasis on the continuity of the council with the preceding tradition.[8] Both Ruini and Marchetto quote in favor of their interpretation a passage from an address Pope John Paul II gave on the occasion of the conference held in the Vatican in 2000 on "The Implementation of Vatican II." The pope's words: "The church has always known the rules for a correct interpretation of the contents of dogma. These rules are woven into the fabric of faith and not outside it. To read the council as if it marked a break with the past, while in fact it placed itself in the line of the faith of all times, is decidedly unacceptable."[9]

Thus an interpretation of the council has emerged that is based on one fundamental assumption: the council was in all important regards continuous with the Catholic past. In fact, that assumption seems to be already well along the road to achieving official and prescriptive status. In 1985, for instance, the synod of bishops that met in the Vatican on the occasion of the 20th anniversary of the closing of the council laid down six norms for its interpretation.[10] When, from the viewpoint of a professional historian, I examine the norms, I have to say that they strike me as resoundingly sound. I will return to them later. At this point, however, I want to highlight number five: "The council must be interpreted in continuity with the great tradition of the church, including other councils."

In any case, the "Bologna School" and especially Alberigo are being singled out as the great propagators of a history of the council that badly distorts it and that must be opposed. Other scholars are also being criticized for a similar approach, but Alberigo and his colleagues are the ones most often mentioned by name. I have studied the five Alberigo volumes. I consider them a remarkable achievement of historical scholarship, and in print I have compared them not to Sarpi but to the authoritative history of the Council of Trent published in the last century by Hubert Jedin.

This is, of course, not to say that the work is perfect. It has, for instance, all the advantages and disadvantages of a collaborative history in which subjects have been parceled out to different authors. Yes, between the lines and sometimes in the lines, one can detect sympathy for "the progressives." But I am generally impressed with the authors' efforts to be fair to the so-called conservatives or minority and especially to be fair to Pope Paul VI, whom they recognized as being in an extraordinarily difficult and delicate situation.

Most important, however, I do not see that Alberigo and others who have used "event" as an instrument to interpret the council have given it the radical meaning that their critics attribute to them. In my opinion, the quotation from John Paul II cannot be applied to Alberigo—nor, for that matter, to any other responsible scholarship I have seen on the council. Nowhere in the Alberigo volumes is there the slightest suggestion that "new beginning" meant in any way a rupture in the faith of the Church or a diminution of any dogma. The only person I know who believed and propagated that assessment was Archbishop Marcel Lefebvre, who declared the council heretical. "New beginning" in any case seems like a weak description compared with "new Pentecost," which is how on December 8, 1962, Pope John XXIII described what he hoped for from the council.[11]

Whatever the merits and demerits of the two sides, this controversy puts before us in a new, clear, and dramatic way a problem that has dogged Vatican II all along: its interpretation. That is certainly not a problem peculiar to the council, but it is particularly acute for it. For one thing, Ruini, Marchetto, and others are correct when they insist that the documents of the council do nothing but insist on the continuity of the council with the tradition of the Church. On the surface there is in the documents no explicit and straightforward indication that any change was being made in procedures, discipline, doctrine, or ecclesiastical style. In this regard, Vatican II is not notably different from the Council of Trent. Nevertheless, it still poses a major interpretative problem, because in the years immediately following Vatican II, we often heard that it was "the end of the Counter Reformation," or even "the end of the Constantinian era," or, indeed, a "new Pentecost." We heard and read a great deal about "the spirit of the council," which seemed to imply a reality that to some extent transcended the letter of its documents and carried with it an implication of, well, a "new beginning" in many areas. The inadequacy of the term "spirit of the council" gradually emerged as it became clear that *your* "spirit of the council" was not *my* "spirit of the council," but many of us, I believe, still cannot shake the feeling that the expression got hold of something that was both real and important. "Spirit" suggested that the council had an overall orientation or pointed in a certain direction.

What is missing in the otherwise excellent norms provided by the synod of 1985 is one that would read somewhat as follows: "While always keeping in mind the fundamental continuity in the great tradition of the Church, interpreters must also take due account of how the council is discontinuous with previous practices, teachings, and traditions, indeed, discontinuous with previous councils." Without such a norm, the emphasis is exclusively on continuity. To thus insist is to blind oneself to discontinuities, which is to blind oneself to change of any kind. And if there is no change, nothing happened. Vatican II was a celebration of the perennial faith of the Catholic Church.

Such continuity, I venture, takes the Church out of history and puts it out of touch with reality as we know it. In Catholicism this emphasis on continuity is not new, but it became characteristic in the 16th century. As I suggested, it found strong expression in the decrees of the Council of Trent, which to an unprecedented degree insisted that they were teaching and prescribing nothing that was not in continuity with the apostolic tradition. The council meant to counter Protestant charges that the Church had deviated from that tradition. Later in the century the emphasis gained momentum with Cesare Baronio's *Ecclesiastical Annales*, written to counter the Lutheran *Magdeburg Centuries*, and, as today's controversy makes clear, it has never since quite lost its hold.[12] A distinguished German

Protestant historian, Gottfried Maron, just a few decades ago went so far as to criticize Hubert Jedin's treatment of the era of Trent for precisely this defect.[13] Yet, historians of Trent and of the Counter Reformation have done little else but tell us how Catholicism changed in the 16th century, to a great extent as a result of the council. Even though Trent insisted on its continuity, something changed. Something happened. Why else would we speak of a "Tridentine era"?

In the late 19th century, Otto von Bismark did not lack reasons to try to bring Catholics to heel in the new German *Reich*, but Vatican I's definitions of papal primacy and especially papal infallibility provided him with yet another reason to launch his *Kulturkampf* against the Church. In 1874 he published a circular letter in which he said, among other things, that the definitions reduced the bishops to mere tools (*Werkzeuge*) of the pope, who now had more power than any absolute monarch of the past. The German bishops' joint statement of early 1875 tried to refute Bismark's allegations, especially by arguing that the definitions had changed nothing, "not the least thing."[14] Pius IX agreed with this interpretation. The definitions, it seems, were a nonevent.

Did anything happen at Vatican II? Anything of significance? I believe something happened, and I will try briefly to say why. I will do so by indicating some of the extraordinary ways the council was discontinuous with the 20 councils that preceded it. I must begin, however, with a big qualification. As a practicing historian I have come to realize that in any social entity the continuities run deeper and tend to be stronger than the discontinuities. The *Annales* school of historiography has taught us well the overriding importance of "la longue durée."[15] After the American Revolution the citizens of the new nation continued to eat the same kind of food, read the same kind of books, think pretty much the same kind of thoughts, founded their nation on principles largely derived from their English experience, and even continued to speak the same English language. Much the same can be said analogously of the French after the bloody trauma of the French Revolution.

Not only in fact but in theory this principle of continuity has to obtain in the Church and obtain in an even more profound way. The mission is to preach the word that was received from the mouth of Christ and the Apostles. The charge to the Church is to hand on that message, not adulterate or change it. I cannot imagine any theologian, any historian, any believer disagreeing with that principle. The Church is by definition a conservative society.

All that having been said, change happens. The American Revolution was more than a series of battles ending in a treaty. It changed things. Change happens even in the Church. Unless we admit that reality, the history of the Church makes no sense and has no relevance. It is reduced to a collection of more or less interesting stories, as the Church sails through the sea of history unaffected by it. Such a sailing is an expression of the historical mind-set R. G. Collingwood identified many years ago as "substantialism," a notion that goes back to classical authors but still affects us.[16] The Church is not, however, a substance but a community of human beings living in time and space. The story of the Church, therefore, is the story of encounters with "the other." In these encounters both parties are affected. As the Church converted "the barbarians," the barbarians influenced the Church.

Most important, change is inherent in the very concept of tradition, which is not an inert body of truths but an incarnated reality. The very transcendence of the message means it can be only imperfectly articulated by any given person or culture. Continuity is postulated, deeper than any discontinuity, yet certain discontinuities and shifts in emphasis seem equally postulated. The tradition is faithfully passed on only when it is rendered engaging and life-giving.

John Courtney Murray said that development of doctrine was "*the* issue under the issues at Vatican II."[17] Although I believe that there was in fact a second, closely related, issue under the issues (the relationship of center to periphery), the current debate over interpretation bears out that that issue is still unresolved and burning. Development is a soft word for change. It presumes continuity. It also presumes discontinuity. I am the same person I was 50 years ago, yet in important ways I am not the same person. Just how continuity and discontinuity function must be discerned in each case, but this tricky relationship cannot be understood by ignoring either factor.

The Council and the Councils

In what ways and to what degree was Vatican II discontinuous with its predecessors and what is the import of that discontinuity? Those are the questions. At the outset it is helpful to recall that almost the only feature common to all the councils from Nicaea (325) to Vatican II is that they have been assemblies, principally of bishops, that have made authoritative decisions binding on the whole Church. Other than that they differ considerably among themselves. They are to a greater or lesser degree discontinuous with one another.

The councils fall into two clearly distinct groups. The first eight were all held in the East, had Greek as their official language, were convoked by the emperor or empress, and no pope attended any of them. The remaining 13 were all held in Italy, France, or Switzerland, conducted in Latin, and were, in one way or another, convoked by the pope. Except for the Council of Florence, there was no notable participation in them by members of the Greek-speaking Church. The councils became an institution of the West—hardly an insignificant change.

Although bishops have for the most part been the determining influence in the councils, others have at times played roles just as important, as with Emperor Charles V at Trent, King Philip IV of France at Vienne, the Empress Irene at Nicaea II, and of course Emperor Constantine at Nicaea. Although some 400 bishops attended Lateran Council IV (1215), they were greatly outnumbered by the 800 abbots who attended. At Lateran V (1512–1517), 26 secular rulers, nobles, and knights are listed as participants, a number that does not include the representatives sent by the great monarchs.

I could go on, but I hope I have made the point that there is no reason to be surprised if Vatican II has distinctive features. What I will try to show, however, is how significant those features are when taken in the aggregate—so significant, in fact, as to require, as Ruini has postulated, a new hermeneutic. But it is a hermeneutic that takes serious account of the discontinuity, thus putting the council's continuity in perspective.

The most obvious of these special characteristics is the massive proportions of Vatican II and its remarkable international breadth. It can with some justification be described as the biggest meeting in the history of the world—not in the sense that it attracted the hundreds of thousands that events like the international Olympics do. It was biggest only if we take into account all the factors that are integral to it, beginning with its length, which must include the two years of intense preparation as well as the four years it was in session. This may not seem long compared with Trent, which stretched over 17 years. But for Trent the number is deceptive because of the long intervals between the three periods in which the council was actually in session.

Unlike other councils the consultation with bishops and others before the council was thorough. It fills 13 folio volumes, well over 7,000 pages. When this material was reworked by the preparatory commissions it amounted to another six volumes and another 4,000 pages. These figures are dwarfed by the 35 volumes of the *acta* of the council itself, which brings the grand total to 54 volumes. All the documents related to Trent, the largest collection for any other council, consist of 17 volumes. Vatican II issued 16 final documents. The pagination of these 16 is almost twice the length of the decrees of Trent, and the decrees of Trent and Vatican II together equal in volume the decrees of all the other 19 councils taken together. Those 16 decrees seem like a spectacularly long-winded way of saying, "Nothing is happening here. Business as usual."

The sheer quantity of the official documentation reflects the immense dimensions of almost every other aspect of the council. Approximately 2,500 bishops participated in the council. In contrast, about 750 bishops were present at Vatican I. The Council of Trent opened with just 29 bishops or prelates and five superiors general of religious orders. Even later, at its best-attended sessions, the number of voting members at Trent barely exceeded 200.

The bishops who actually attended Vatican II came from 116 different countries, whereas 40 percent of the bishops at Vatican I were from Italy. Many brought with them a secretary or a theologian, or both. To this number must be added others who came to Rome because of official or semiofficial business related to the council, which, of course, included about a hundred "observers" from other churches, as well as representatives of the media. By the time the council opened, the Vatican had issued about a thousand press cards to journalists. Probably close to 10,000 people were present in Rome at any given time during the council because they had some kind of business relating to it.

It would be a terrible shame, and surprising, if this unprecedented expenditure of time, effort, and money (which I have not even mentioned) eventuated in nothing other than "business as usual." Yet two more features about the participants in Vatican II deserve mention. The first is not only the presence but the highly influential role of some Roman Catholic theologians who, even as the council opened, were under a ban of silence imposed on them by the Vatican's Holy Office of the Inquisition and whose views had in one way or another been condemned. As the council got under way, these theologians not only had the ban on them implicitly lifted but went on to be among the principal architects of the council's decrees. I am referring, of course, to theologians like Yves Congar, Henri de Lubac, Karl Rahner, and the American John Courtney Murray. This feature of the council, too, was not only unprecedented but surely suggests that something was happening at the council that was—or wanted to be—a change in the status quo.

The second feature is the presence of the observers, honored guests who did not share many of the basic principles out of which the Catholic Church operated and were invited to make their differences known, which they did outside the formal sessions of the council. Unprecedented. The presence of the observers stimulated a more searching scrutiny of the deliberations and decisions of the council, but it was also important for nudging the council to consider issues of concern to others besides Roman Catholics—or, maybe better, besides Roman Catholic prelates.

The interest in the council of the communications media was aggressive. This, too, helped the nudging process. Until the Council of Trent the deliberations of councils were almost exclusively the private concern of those who participated in them. The invention of printing that ushered in a new situation. By the time of Vatican II radio and television could transmit news around the world at the very moment any newsworthy event happened. Once the council got under way what particularly captivated the attention of the media and the public they served was the ill-kept secret of the sometimes acrid debates and confrontations in the council and the emerging possibility of changes in posture and practice that just a short while before had seemed set in stone. The Catholic Church had presented itself internally and to the world at large as the Church that did not change. It took great care to show a united front on all issues and to deal swiftly with any phenomena within the Church that might seem to suggest otherwise. Yet the debates and disagreements in the council, despite efforts to hide or disguise them, were manifest and entered the public forum, where they were discussed and debated. They shocked some, gave delight to others, and rendered patent to all that Catholicism was not the monolith they thought they knew.

The new ease of communication meant that after the council was over its decisions could be implemented with a speed and directness no previous council could come close to mustering, even if it had wanted to. In fact, with only a very few exceptions the decisions of previous councils had no immediate relevance for the life of the faithful or at least did not entail a wrenching change in received patterns. As it turned out, some decisions of Vatican II made a dramatic impact on the life of ordinary believers. When such believers entered their churches for Mass a year or so after the council, for instance, they experienced something so different from what they had experienced all their lives up to that Sunday that they would have had to be deaf, dumb, and blind not to notice it.

The decisions of previous councils were directed almost exclusively to the clergy. Vatican II departed from that pattern by addressing Catholics of every status. Most remarkable was the attention it paid to the laity. Then in *Gaudium et spes* it addressed "all humanity," all persons of good will—Christians and non-Christians, believers and nonbelievers. Vatican II thus took greater account of the world around it than any previous council and assumed as one of its principal tasks dialogue or conversation with that world in order to work for a better world, not simply a better Church. It dealt with war, peace, poverty, family, and similar topics as they touched every human being. This is a breathtaking change in scope from that of every previous council.

Aggiornamento and *Ressourcement*

Whence the impulse that allowed such change as legitimate and good? The mentality with which many of the most influential bishops and theologians approached their task was, despite the condemnations issued during the Modernist crisis of the early 20th century, more historical than in any previous council. This mentality, the result of the great impetus to historical studies that began in the 19th century and never abated, had in certain Catholic circles deeply affected the study of every aspect of church life and doctrine. The leading voices at the council were thus quite aware of the changes that had taken place in the long history of the Church and were willing to draw consequences from them. This keener sense of history permitted greater freedom in judging that some practices, traditions, or doctrinal formulations might simply be anachronistic or currently inappropriate or even harmful and therefore should be modified or eliminated.

This persuasion found expression in two words that capture the justification or motivation behind many of the council's actions: the Italian *aggiornamento* and the French *ressourcement*. Although they express almost diametrically opposed impulses—the first looking forward, the second backward—they are both geared to change. *Aggiornamento* means updating or, more boldly, modernizing. John XXIII's opening allocution to the council fathers provided a basis for it, which was soon taken up by the progressive wing.[18] Changes needed to be made in the Church to make it more viable in the "new era" that the council assumed was dawning. On one level this was nothing new. Lateran IV legitimated changes if they were done out of *urgens necessitas vel evidens utilitas.*[19]

But at least three aspects were special about the *aggiornamento* of Vatican II. First, the changes done in the name of *aggiornamento* were sometimes obvious reversals of what had broadly been considered normative. Second, no previous council ever took the equivalent of *aggiornamento* as a leitmotif, as a broad principle rather than as a rare exception, with its implication that the Church should change in certain regards to meet the times rather than the times change to meet the Church. Nevertheless, the bishops at the council had no intention of rupturing the fundamental continuity of the Catholic tradition. In the opening oration at Lateran V (1512), Egidio da Viterbo in an often quoted axiom expressed the mind-set that prevailed in councils up to Vatican II: we are to be changed by religion, he insisted, not religion by us.[20] The bishops at Vatican II surely subscribed to that principle, but they would interpret it in an unprecedentedly broad way.

- Third, the council took as axiomatic that Catholicism was adaptive even to "the modern world." This was a shift from the integralism that marked most Catholic thinking from the early 19th century well into the 20th and saw almost everything stemming from the Enlightenment and the French Revolution as incompatible with the Church. How and why this shift took place is difficult to determine satisfactorily, but in a few circles it was already under way by the 1920s. Jacques Maritain's *Antimoderne* (1922) was, despite the title, a catalyst and a symptom of it. According to him, Catholicism possesses a "bold ability to adapt itself to the new conditions erupting suddenly in the life of the world."[21]

- *Ressourcement* means return to the sources with a view to making changes that retrieve a more normative past. It has *avant la lettre* a truly venerable history that has found explicit and important articulation in the history of the Western Church beginning with the Gregorian Reform of the eleventh century when a series of reforming popes spearheaded a vigorous campaign to restore a more ancient canonical tradition. As the dust began to settle after the bitter and bloody battles that the campaign ignited, the principle, even though not explicitly invoked, undergirded much of the important legislation of Lateran Councils I and II regarding especially the election of bishops and clerical celibacy.[22]

Ressourcement was in its Latin form, *ad fontes*, the motto of the great humanist movement of the Renaissance. *Ad fontes*—a call to return to the good literature of antiquity to displace the Latin jargon or doggerel, as the humanists saw it, of "the schools," that is, the universities. It was a call to recover a more literary style of discourse. Included in the canon of good literature were not only Demosthenes and Cicero but the Bible and the fathers of the church as well.

This "return to the sources" is what drove humanists like Petrarch and Erasmus because they believed that the recuperation of the ancient authors had profound ethical, religious, and theological implications. *Ressourcement* also drove the Protestant Reformers, as they sought to restore the authentic gospel that the papal Church had obscured and perverted. In Catholicism in the 19th century, *ressourcement* lay behind both Leo XIII's encyclical *Aeterni patris* (1879) initiating the Thomistic revival, as well as the conservative origins of the liturgical movement with Prosper Guéranger in the monastery of Solemnes.

On the eve of Vatican II *ressourcement* drove much of the theological ferment in France that caused grave concern in Rome and elicited from the Holy Office silencings and condemnations. Stigmatized by its opponents as *la nouvelle théologie*, it was viewed by its proponents as just the opposite, as a recovery of an older theology—to a large extent, the theology of the fathers.[23] The problem was that this *ressourcement* seemed to contravene the earlier Thomistic and, more broadly, neo-Scholastic *ressourcement* that originated with Leo XIII and that now monopolized Catholic theological discourse. In *Humani generis* Pius XII expressed his displeasure at those who criticized Thomism and wanted "to bring about a return in the explanation of Catholic doctrine to the way of speaking used in Holy Scripture and the Fathers of the Church."[24] Within a short time proponents of the "new" theology were being removed from their teaching posts.[25]

Ad fontes and *ressourcement*—these catchwords are, on the surface, about discontinuity. By the time of Vatican II even the most conservative theologians admitted that some form of "development" had taken place in the teaching of the Church through the centuries. Newman's *Essay* on the subject, received with suspicion in Catholic circles when first published, was now taken as its virtually definitive exposition. But "development" was usually understood as moving further along a given path, as with the definition of the dogma of the Assumption following the definition of the Immaculate Conception and leading to the hope expressed by many on the eve of Vatican II for further Marian definitions at the council. *Ressourcement* is not quite the same thing. It looks to the past for norms or practices or mind-sets that somehow are going to change or correct or at least qualify the direction of current developments.

This "return to the sources" has itself had different modalities. With the Gregorian reformers of the eleventh century it said: we have been on the wrong path by letting laymen choose bishops; we must stop that and return to the right path of canonical elections; we are not going to continue to move along path X but go back to the fork in the road and now, instead, take path Y. Confrontation, war, and the sacking of Rome followed. Eventually the Gregorians were forced to accommodate their goals to the political reality of their day. Nonetheless, in principle their "return" postulated a radical discontinuity.

The *ressourcement* of the mid-20th century was not quite the same thing. It was more multiform. It is possible to include within it, for instance, Thomists like Marie-Dominique Chenu as well as patristic scholars like de Lubac and Jean Daniélou.[26] It was reacting in the first place to the rigid propositional theology of the seminary textbooks and to the narrowing and enervating of the Catholic tradition that the scholars of the *ressourcement* believed those texts effected. It was reacting to the ahistorical mentality of those texts.[27] The recovery of the patristic mode, along with a recovery of a more genuine Thomism, was a return to the life-giving wellsprings. It would show forth the richness of the Catholic tradition and at the same time suggest that the tradition was bigger than any system. It would thus suggest that mystery was the first quality of the tradition.

Opponents of the *nouvelle théologie* did not see *ressourcement* that way. They saw it as subversive of the status quo on just about every level. Such a return would introduce unacceptable, indeed heterodox, discontinuities into the tradition. That is why applications of the *ressourcement* principle often ran into trouble at Vatican II. The lightening rod at the council was collegiality. Its advocates justified it as a venerable tradition that needed to be recovered to complement and "develop" the teaching of Vatican I on the hierarchical structure of the Church and even to enhance the prerogatives of the papacy. Its opponents saw it not as developing Vatican I but as contravening it.[28] Hence the bitter struggles over it during Vatican II.

The principle ran into trouble in other ways, but for our purposes the most crucial is one that has received practically no attention despite its profound importance for understanding the council and constructing a "new hermeneutic" for it. I am speaking of the literary form in which the decrees of the council were framed. Like collegiality that aspect of *ressourcement* ran into considerable opposition especially in the early months of the council, but it eventually prevailed. It must be taken into account if we are to know whether anything happened at Vatican II.

Genre, Form, Content

What happened at Vatican II? That question is usually answered by indicating how certain elements in the key decrees were discontinuous with previous teaching or practice. *Unitatis redintegratio,* the decree on ecumenism, was discontinuous not only with the polemics of the Counter-Reformation but more pointedly with the encyclicals *Mortalium animos* of Pius XI (1928) condemning the ecumenical movement and *Humani generis* of Pius XII (1950) condemning "eirenicism."[29] It was discontinuous with the mind-set that as late as 1963 forbade a nun in a Catholic hospital to summon a Protestant minister for a dying person.[30] *Dei Verbum,* the Constitution on the Word of God, was discontinuous with the tradition that since the 16th century had made the Bible practically a forbidden book for Catholics.[31] *Dignitatis humanae,* the declaration on religious liberty, was discontinuous not only with the long "Constantinian era" but particularly with the condemnations of separation of church and state by the popes of the 19th and 20th centuries. On the very eve of Vatican II, John Courney Murray was in difficulties with the Holy Office for questioning that the Catholic confessional state was the ideal to be striven for.[32]

These and similar changes were strenuously opposed in the council by a minority precisely because they were changes. They are immensely significant but also well known and frequently commented on. They can be called changes in content. I am asking, however, that we shift the focus from content to form. Even though message and medium are one reality, I am asking that in so far as it is possible we shift the focus from *what* the council said to *how* it said it. This means engaging in form-analysis. It means taking into account the most obvious feature of the council's 16 documents and drawing conclusions from it.

What is that feature? Their length. Why are they so long? Because, as was repeatedly insisted upon in the council, they are "pastoral." This so-called pastoral form is a literary genre that was new to the conciliar tradition; it was a distincively new mode of discourse. That fact is crucially important for understanding what went on in the council. Form and content—*verba et res*—cannot be separated. There is no understanding a poem without taking into account that it is a poem. In our case the form or genre results in a council different from every one that preceded it. The council adopted a new style of discourse and in so doing set forth through that style a striking teaching on how the Church was to be.

The Traditional Genres

Through the centuries councils have made use of a range of literary forms. Beginning with Nicaea, however, the vast majority of those genres evince characteristics derived from the legislative-judicial traditions of discourse developed in the Roman empire. These genres were primarily laws or judicial sentences. It is not far off the mark to postulate that the implicit model for the early Church's synods and councils was the Roman senate.[33] Although that body had lost much of its authority by the time Constantine assumed a leadership role in the Church, it continued to legislate both in Rome and in its counterpart in Constantinople, where Constantine presided over it.

When Constantine convoked the Council of Nicaea, he held it there in his palace. He acted as a kind of honorary president of the assembly and intervened in its deliberations. He ratified the council's decisions by making them legally binding and, except where they would impinge on the rights and duties of bishops, took responsibility for their implementation. A pattern was set. At the Council of Chalcedon (451), the emperor's 19 envoys sat on a dais in the center of the assembly and, though they did not vote, they chaired the meeting and set the order of the day.

While assuring correct belief in the Church and appropriate behavior especially of the clergy were the council's fundamental concerns, they were not and could not be separated from securing the proper social order at large and hence from their implementation by the civil authorities. Law and order. From the beginning that enforcement was inconsistent, depending on the whim of the emperors, but coercive enforcement by emperors, kings, and other lay magnates continued to be a constitutive element of councils down to Vatican I (1870), by which time it had become politically unfeasible because of the growing separation of church and state.

The fundamental assumption governing councils from their very inception, therefore, was that they were legislative bodies that issued ordinances regarding doctrinal formulations and public behavior—*fides et mores*. To these ordinances were often attached penalties for violators. The very first canon of Nicaea imposed suspension on any cleric who castrated himself.[34] The first canon of the next council, Constantinople I (381), anathematized all heresies (a long list of them followed).[35]

Among the literary forms councils used were confessions of faith, historical narratives, bulls and letters, judicial sentences against ecclesiastical criminals, constitutions, "chapters," and various kinds of "decrees." Especially in the early councils the most respected and important form was the creedal statement. Nonetheless, down through the centuries the canon stands out for its recurrence and—if we take into account that in the sources it sometimes goes by other names—for its numerical predominance over every other form. A canon is an ordinance, usually only a few lines in length, that entails punishment for failure to comply.[36] It is a form that clearly manifests the assumption that a council is a legislative-judicial body. Vatican I, for instance, issued 18 canons, whereas Trent issued more than 130 for its doctrinal decrees alone and did much the same for its disciplinary enactments. The canons generally employ the formula: "If anyone should . . . , let him be anathema."

Even dogmatic canons do not strike directly at what a person might believe or think or feel, but at what they "say" or "deny," that is, at some observable behavior. As such, they are not concerned with interiority. Like any good law, canons and their equivalents were formulated to be as unambiguous as possible. They drew clear lines. They spoke a language that tried unmistakably to distinguish "who's in" and "who's out," which often entailed not only meting out punishment for the latter but even considering them enemies.

The language of the councils, of which the canon was emblematic, could be vehement in its depiction of those who presumably were subverting the Church, whether by propagating bad belief or indulging in bad behavior. The language is adversarial, the language of battle against a foe. To that extent it is a departure from the sober language of the courts. At Vienne (1311–1312) the council condemned the Knights Templar in the language of "anger and wrath" reminiscent of the prophets.[37] Pope Julius II's decree in Lateran V (1512) against the cardinals who had attempted to depose him minced no words: "We condemn, reject and detest, with the approval of this holy council, each and every thing done by those sons of perdition."[38] The Council of Constance (1418) denounced John Wyclif as a "profligate enemy" of the faith and a "pseudo-Christian," and handed over his disciple Jan Hus to be burned at the stake.[39]

• My point is that, although allowances must be made for many differences, the councils from Nicaea to Vatican I had a characteristic style of discourse. The style was composed of two basic elements. The first was a literary genre—the canon or its equivalent. The second was the vocabulary typical of the genre and appropriate to it. It consisted in words of threat and intimidation, words of surveillance and punishment, words of a superior speaking to inferiors, or, just as often, to an enemy. It consisted in power-words.

All this sounds grim. It might sound devoid of even the slightest concern for the spirit, a good case of the letter killing. We need, however, to employ here a hermeneutic of compassion and acknowledge that even in the church surveillance and punishment is sometimes the only practical course of action if we want to change behavior. The bishops at Trent could not reform the episcopacy (that is, themselves) without strong sanctions. They knew this, and they acted accordingly.[40] We need also recognize that changing behavior can sometimes result in a change of heart—working from the outside to the inside. Although canons and the like deal with the exterior, in so far as they are inspired by Christian principles they must be presumed not to be entirely devoid of relationship to inner conversion.

Be that as it may, this style of discourse expressed and promoted procedures in accord with a certain style of being and behavior. The decrees of Trent illustrate the point. Despite the council's achievements, inconceivable without the "language-game" the council adopted, in the long run the decrees reinforced "social disciplining" as an ecclesiastical style and promoted an image of the Church as a stern, exigent, and suspicious parent.[41] "Behave thus . . . . or else." The language projected the image, and the image promoted the reality and helped it self-fulfill.

In the 19th century that reality expressed itself with insistence and prominence at the highest level in the style of papal pronouncements, such as Gregory XVI's *Mirari vos* (1832), Pius IX's "Syllabus of Errors" (1864), and in the early 20th century Pius X's *Lamentabili* and *Pascendi* (1907). The language of these documents and the many like them is the language of adversarial relationships. "We would have drowned," said Gregory, "as a result of the terrible conspiracy of impious men . . . so that we had to restrain their great obstinacy with the rod. . . . Depravity exults, science is impudent, liberty dissolute. The holiness of the sacred is despised . . . and errors of all kinds spread boldly." The errors Gregory especially meant were freedom of the press, liberty of conscience, separation of church and state, and, not least, rebellion against monarchs by "shameless lovers of freedom."[42] By the time Vatican II opened vituperation of such high quality had practically disappeared from ecclesiastical statements but not the adversarial stance. Even the sober canon assumed bad will on the part of persons contravening it.

From the beginning concepts from Greek philosophy also affected conciliar language, but especially in the High Middle Ages the dialectical and analytical aspects of that tradition began to play a greater role. Dialectics is the art of proving a point and thus winning an argument. It is an appeal to the mind. It cannot succeed without a technical vocabulary and unambiguous definitions. It thus draws clear lines of demarcation and in so doing manifests that characteristic of the legal-judicial tradition. The decrees of Trent on the sacraments are perhaps the best examples of this tradition in action in the councils, but the assumption that the purpose of councils is "to define" betrays the broader influence of the dialectical tradition.

The New Genre

The first open clash at Vatican II between the progressives and conservatives took place in mid-November 1962, over the document on "The Sources of Revelation" (*De fontibus revelationis*). The document's style was a bone of contention. Besides other traits of the legislative-judicial style, the document contained expressions like "Let no one dare say . . ." and "The church utterly condemns. . . ."[43] At that early moment in the council, Cardinal Alfredo Ottaviani, prefect of the Holy Office and chief architect of the document, felt compelled to defend it precisely against the anticipated criticism that its style was not "pastoral." In his presentation of the document to the council, he correctly insisted that its style was "the style that has been sanctioned by its use through the ages."[44]

Ottaviani was defensive because a month earlier, on October 22, the day that substantive discussion opened in the council, style was already an issue. The council fathers had been presented with their first schema, *Sacrosanctum concilium*. Cardinal Josef Frings was the first speaker, and almost the first words out of his mouth were: "The schema is to be commended for its modest and pastoral literary style, full of the spirit of Holy Scripture and the fathers of the church."[45] In fact, that document less well exemplified "the spirit of the fathers of the church" than the revised versions of other documents that came later, but Frings rang the bell announcing what was to come. It was a bell announcing the legitimizing of a style that only a decade earlier *Humani generis* had dismissed as illegitimate.

• During the first period of the council (1962), the progressives continued to insist on a "pastoral" style. On November 19 Bishop Emiel-Jozef De Smedt, speaking for the Secretariate for Promoting Christian Unity, made an important intervention criticizing *De fontibus*. What, he asked, is required to foster greater unity among Christians today? Of course, clear and precise presentation of positions. But just as important is an appropriate style of presentation, a style that will foster genuine dialogue. That is precisely what this schema lacks, framed as it is in Scholastic categories. "On the contrary, the biblical and patristic style in and of itself avoids and prevents many difficulties, minunderstandings, and prejudices."[46]

Ottaviani's brief and angry presentation to the council of the schema *De ecclesia* some ten days later betrays how frayed tempers had become over precisely this point of style: "The concern of those who prepared the schema was that it be as pastoral as possible. . . . I say this because I expect to hear the usual litany from the fathers of the council: it's academic, it's not ecumenical, it's not pastoral, it's negative and other things like that. . . . Those whose constant cry is 'Take it away! Take it away!' are ready to open fire."[47] That very day De Smedt accepted the challenge and opened fire by denouncing the schema for a style that was triumphal, clerical, and juridical.[48] His speech became one of the most quoted of the council.

• Style was, therefore, an explicit and important issue. The new style did not slip into the council unnoticed. By the second period (1963), the opponents of the change had been forced to to capitulate, but not without still nagging criticism. The council had adopted for its pronouncements a new style of discourse, a new genre. That style, while operative in all 16 final documents, is best exemplified in the four constitutions of the council—on the liturgy, the Church, revelation, and the Church in the modern world. Even in the constitutions, however, the new style suffers interruptions, deviations, and admixtures. Long sections are simply expository, but the genre still frames them.

The genre can be precisely identified. It was a genre known and practiced in many cultures from time immemorial, but it was clearly analyzed and its features carefully codified by classical authors like Aristotle, Cicero, and Quintilian.[49] It is the panegyric, that is, the painting of an idealized portrait in order to excite admiration and appropriation. An old genre in the rhetorical tradition of the West, it was used extensively by the fathers of the church in their homilies and other writings. It derives from neither the legal tradition of classical antiquity nor the philosophical/dialectical but from the humanistic or literary.

I have tried in my *Four Cultures of the West* to delineate the characteristics of these traditions and point to some of their religious manifestations in some detail.[50] Also pertinent is my earlier study of the sermons preached *coram papa* in the Sistine Chapel during the Renaissance.[51] In it I show how the introduction of classical rhetoric in the form of the epideictic oration changed the ethos, purpose, and content of preaching there, moving it from its medieval and Scholastic form to something quite different. The appropriation of the epideictic genre redefined what a sermon was supposed to do: rather than proving points, it was now to touch hearts and move hearers to action for their fellow human beings. Like any good oration these, of course, "taught," but in a different mode than did the Scholastic sermons.

This phenomenon was part of the Renaissance's general revival of interest in the fathers whom, until recently, scholars have neglected—a revival of interest that manifests striking parallels with the patristic *ressourcement* of the mid-20th century. Erasmus, so scorned by theologians on both sides of the confessional divide down to our own day, produced his magnificent editions of the Greek and Latin fathers and sought thereby to renew theology and Christian devotion. This renewal entailed adoption of the rhetorical style of the fathers for religious and theological discourse.[52] The movement had its origins in Italy, however, where it was received with more appreciation and serenity than it was in northern Europe.[53]

The bitter polemics of the Reformation and Counter-Reformation obliterated the memory of this important moment in Christian discourse, so that today historians of theology move directly from the late Middle Ages to the Reformation without passing through the Renaissance. My research on it, however, is responsible for my recurring experience of *déja vu* in reading the documents of Vatican II and for my recognizing how the principles of epideictic rhetoric are operative in them.

How did Vatican II come to adopt the epideictic form? The model was at hand. The patristic revival went back to the 19th century. Jacques-Paul Migne had finished publishing his *Patrologia latina* (1844–1865) well over a decade before Leo XIII's encyclical on Aquinas. In 1943, however, the revival received an important goad when Daniélou and de Lubac began publishing *Sources chrétiennes*. As Brian Daley says: "The Fathers were, both for the first editors of *Sources chrétiennes* and their critics, an emblem for a new, different way of thinking and speaking about the central realities of the Christian faith."[54]

The first document to come to the floor of the council that rather consistently employed this "new way of thinking and speaking" was the revised version of the Dogmatic Constitution on the Church, *Lumen gentium*. It can hardly be a coincidence that the titles of the first and last chapters of de Lubac's *Méditation sur l'église* (1953) are identical with the corresponding chapters of *Lumen gentium*, and that his other chapter titles are loosely congruent with key aspects of *Lumen gentium*.[55] *Méditation* was written in a style strongly evocative of the poetical-rhetorical style of the fathers.

"The Mystery of the Church" is the title for the opening chapter of *Lumen gentium* and the title for the opening chapter of de Lubac's book. In January 1963, in the name of the Coordinating Commission of the council, Cardinal Suenens had directed the committee revising the original *De ecclesia* to make the mystery of the Church the opening chapter of the new text. He had earlier in the commission criticized the original document for using an inappropriate genre.[56]

Gérard Philips, not de Lubac, was principally responsible for the revision. But no matter how little or how much de Lubac's book directly influenced the development of *Lumen gentium*, the document was written in the same style and opened with "mystery," something beyond definition. It thus moved the council away from what councils were expected to do—define. Instead, the document raised up before our eyes Christ, God, the Church, and the dignity of our human nature to excite us to wonder and admiration. It did this through a panorama of images, evocative of the warmth and richness of the reality of the Church. It engaged in a rhetoric of praise and congratulation. It engaged in panegyric, in the *ars laudandi*, whose technical name is "epideictic."

The purpose of the genre, therefore, is not so much to clarify concepts as to heighten appreciation for a person, an event, an institution, and to excite emulation of an ideal. If most Fourth of July speeches are secular examples of the genre at its worst, Lincoln's Gettysburg Address is an example of it at its best.[57] Lincoln tried simply to raise appreciation for what was at stake in the war and, at least by implication, to praise it as noble and worthy of the great cost. He wanted to touch the affect of his audience by holding up ideals whose attractiveness would motivate them to strive to achieve them. He employed a rhetoric of invitation.

The documents of Vatican II fit this mold. That is their "style." They hold up ideals and then often draw conclusions from them and spell out consequences, as with the decree on bishops in which their responsibilities are clearly laid out. The responsibilities are laid out, however, not as a code of conduct to be enforced but as ideal to be striven for, with the understanding that they are to be adapted to times and circumstances. Trent had proportionately more to say about bishops than did Vatican II, but it did so through ordinances. Although it is possible to derive an ideal beneath the ordinances, the surface message is the enforcement of law and order.[58]

The epideictic genre is a form of the art of persuasion and thus of reconciliation. While it raises appreciation, it creates or fosters among those it addresses a realization that they all share (or should share) the same ideals and need to work together to achieve them. This genre reminds people of what they have in common rather than what might divide them, and the reminder motivates them to cooperate in enterprises for the common good, to work for a common cause.

To engage in persuasion is to some extent to put oneself on the same level as those being persuaded. Persuaders do not command from on high. Otherwise they would not be persuading but coercing. Persuasion works from the inside out. In order to persuade, persuaders need to establish an identity between themselves and their audience and to make them understand that they share the same concerns. They share, indeed, the same "joy and hope, the same grief and anguish."[59]

The form prompts and enhances congruent content. It should come as no surprise that reconciliation has been one of the perennial themes of the epideictic genre. Although ecumenism of some form was on the agenda of Vatican II from the moment John XXIII announced the council, it found appropriate expression in the new genre and could feel very much at home there. Since the genre wants to raise its audience to big issues, its content in a Christian context is typically the major doctrines of creation, redemption, sanctification.

Implicit in this penchant of the genre to focus on big issues is an invitation to rise above all pettiness and to strive for an expansive vision and a generous spirit. In fact, magnanimity was a virtue especially extolled by the classical masters of the rhetorical tradition, intent as they were on motivating individuals to make great sacrifices to promote the common good. Cicero gave eloquent expression to it in his *De officiis* (I.20.66). It was taken up by Christian authors, including Thomas Aquinas, but, not surprisingly, it was most characteristically praised in the Renaissance. In the Jesuit *Constitutions*, Ignatius Loyola commended it as one of the qualities required in the superior general of the order (no. 728).

Those are some of the traits of the genre, and those are the traits that characterize the discourse of Vatican II. The council was about persuading and inviting. To attain that end it used principally the epideictic genre. I am, of course, not saying that the bishops and theologians self-consciously adopted a specific genre of classical rhetoric as such. I am saying that the documents of the council, for whatever reason, fit that pattern and therefore need to be interpreted accordingly.

As with the traditional genres used by councils, the most concrete manifestation of the character of this genre, and therefore an important key to interpreting its import, is the vocabulary it adopts and fosters. Nowhere is that vocabulary more significant than in Vatican II and nowhere is the contrast greater between it and all preceding councils. Nowhere is the vocabulary more indicative of what the genre stands for and therefore of the style of Church the council promoted by means of it.

We must therefore look at words. First, what kind of words are absent? Notably missing are words of alienation, exclusion, enmity, words of threat and intimidation, words of surveillance and punishment. Anathema does not appear a single time. Although the hierarchical character of the Church is repeatedly stressed and the prerogatives of the supreme pontiff reiterated almost obsessively, the Church is never described as a monarchy nor the members of the Church as subjects. That is a significant departure from previous practice.

What kind of words are present? Words new to conciliar vocabulary, or at least untypical of it. None of them can be considered casual asides or mere window dressing—"mere rhetoric." They are used far too insistently and too characteristically for that. They do not occur here and there but are an across-the-board phenomenon, appearing in all or almost all the final documents. They are the best indicators for getting at that elusive thing, "the spirit of the council." They make it possible for us to escape from the proof-texting that has beset the documents of Vatican II and allow us to rise to patterns and overall orientation. The genre and the vocabulary provide us with that much sought-after "horizon of interpretation." They provide us with the materials to devise what Cardinal Ruini is calling for, a new hermeneutic.

I will divide the words into categories, but the categories are imperfectly distinct from one another. They overlap and crisscross, making the same or related points. They are all, moreover, consonant with the epideictic genre and with the wider rhetorical tradition. Genre and vocabulary taken together constitute and manifest a style of discourse, which almost by definition manifests the style—the how—of the person speaking. In this instance the person speaking is the Church.

One category is made up of horizontal words. Words like "brothers and sisters" stress and give color to the wide range of horizontal relationships that characterize the Church. They contrast with the vertical or top-down words typical of former councils and of the 19th-century papacy. The most widely invoked of such horizontal words after the council and the one that remains best known, despite its problematic implications, is "people of God."

Among the horizontal words are the reciprocity words, such as "cooperation," "partnership," and "collaboration." Striking in *Gaudium et spes* is the bald statement that just as the world learns from the Church the Church learns from the world—in this case, from the *modern* world.[60] But in this horizontal-reciprocity category the two most significant words are "dialogue" and "collegiality." There is scarcely a page in the council documents on which "dialogue" or its equivalent does not occur. "Dialogue" manifests a radical shift form the prophetic I-say-unto-you style that earlier prevailed and indicates something other than unilateral decision-making. "Collegiality," as mentioned, did not find its way into the council's vocabulary without a fierce battle. Implicit in these reciprocity-words, moreover, is engagement and even initiative In the document on the laity, for instance, the council tells them that they have the right and sometimes the duty to make their opinions known.[61] Implicitly the reciprocity words are empowerment words.

Closely related to reciprocity words are friendship words. The most striking is the all-inclusive "human family" to which *Gaudium et spes* is addressed. Similarly related are the humility-words, beginning with the description of the Church as pilgrim. Among the redefinitions the council silently effected is what it did in some passages with the triad prophet-priest-king, where prophet becomes partner in dialogue, priesthood is extended to all believers, and king is defined as servant.[62] The triad was applied to everybody in the Church, laity as well as clergy, and appears in document after document. Servant is not a power-word.

Even though the word "change" (*mutatio*) occurs in the first paragraph of the decree on the liturgy, the first document approved by the council, the Catholic allergy to it prevails elsewhere. A remarkable feature of the vocabulary of the council, nonetheless, is its employment of words that in fact indicate change—words like "development," "progress," and even "evolution." "Pilgrim" perhaps should also be included here. The most familiar change-word associated with Vatican II is the innocent sounding *aggiornamento*.

No doubt, it can be interpreted in a minimal and traditional sense, probably the sense John XXIII intended, but when framed within the full context of the council it becomes one more indicator of a more historical and therefore relativized and open-ended approach to issues and problems. It implies the inevitability of further change in the future and suggests that the council itself must be interpreted in an open-ended way. The council cannot be interpreted and implemented as if it said "thus far and no further." It did not "define."

The final category to which I will call attention is interiority-words. "Joy and hope, grief and anguish"—these are the famous words opening *Gaudium et spes*. The document goes on: for disciples of Christ nothing that is human fails to find an echo in their hearts. Yes, in their hearts. Vatican II was about the inward journey. It was about holiness. Perhaps the most remarkable aspect of *Lumen gentium* is chapter five, "The Call to Holiness." *Lumen gentium* set the agenda, leading the way for the call to holiness to become a great theme of the documents of the council.

Holiness is what the Church is all about. An old truth this, of course, but no previous council had ever explicitly asserted it and certainly never developed it so repeatedly and at such length. It is a call to something more than external conformity to enforceable codes of conduct. It is a call that, though it may have an external form, is, as the documents describe it, related more immediately to the outpouring of the Spirit into the hearts of the faithful, to their free and willing acceptance of the gospel, and to their commitment to service of others in the world.

In this regard the council's emphasis on conscience as the ultimate norm in moral choice is remarkable: "Deep within their conscience individuals discover a law that they do not make for themselves but that they are bound to obey, whose voice, ever summoning them to love and to do what is good and avoid what is evil rings in their hearts."[63] While Catholics must take full and serious account of church teachings and guidance, they must ultimately be guided by the inner law. Preachers, theologians, and saints have always taught in some form or other this primacy of conscience, but no council had ever said it.

I will summarize in a simple litany some of the elements in the change in style of the Church indicated by the council's vocabulary: from commands to invitations, from laws to ideals, from threats to persuasion, from coercion to conscience, from monologue to conversation, from ruling to serving, from withdrawn to integrated, from vertical and top-down to horizontal, from exclusion to inclusion, from hostility to friendship, from static to changing, from passive acceptance to active engagement, from prescriptive to principled, from defined to open-ended, from behavior-modification to conversion of heart, from the dictates of law to the dictates of conscience, from external conformity to the joyful pursuit of holiness.

When those elements are taken in the aggregate, they indicate a model of spirituality. This, they say, is what good Catholics should look like and this is how they should behave. That means the elements indicate what the Church should look like and how it should behave. This is a significant model-shift. This is a teaching of the council. Moreover, those elements taken in the aggregate seem to express something that can be called "the spirit of the council." By examining "the letter" in this way we are able to arrive at "the spirit." The medium in its genre and vocabulary conveys a remarkably coherent message that transcends the particularities of the documents. The form conveys content.

The documents of the council are not literary masterpieces. They are committee documents forged in the heat of debate and disagreement, filled with compromises, misleading euphemisms, and stylistic inconsistencies. Yet, despite their many and obvious weaknesses, they in their most characteristic expressions pertain to a literary genre, and, as such, evince a literary unity. It is new that a council would take care to imbue its statements with vocabulary and themes that cut across all of them. The documents of Vatican II are not a grab-bag collection of ordinances. They cohere with one another.

"The spirit of the council!" Although it is a problematic concept, the bishops' synod of 1985 does not hesitate to use it. I suggested earlier that it meant something like a general orientation. I think my analysis substantiates that meaning, but I believe that in the context of Vatican II the concept is even richer. The council has a spirit because in its most profound reality it was about our "spirit," our souls.

It was about the wellsprings of our motivation, about our call to holiness, about, therefore, spirituality. It provided a profile of the holy Christian as well as the motivation and means to actualize it.

Every one of the elements in my litany above needs qualifications. No institution, for instance, can be simply "open-ended." Sooner or later closure is required. No institution can be all-inclusive. And so forth. Most especially, the horizontal words of the council must be balanced by the vertical. Both are strongly present, and both must be taken into account. In any case, the horizontal words are not about a diminishment of papal or episcopal authority, which the council time and again confirmed, but they are about how that authority is exercised. To that extent the litany as a whole conveys the sweep of the style of the Church that the Second Vatican Council held up for contemplation, admiration, and actualization.

The council's rejection of the style in which preparatory documents like *De ecclesia* and *De fontibus* were composed was not about esthetics. Nor was it just about replacing a theological method. It was about something much more profound: a rejection of ways of thinking, feeling, and behaving of which style was the emblem and engine. It was the rejection of a whole mental and emotional framework that found expression in genre and vocabulary. Style in this sense is not an ornament, not a superficial affectation, but expression of deepest personality. It is the ultimate expression of meaning. *Le style, c'est l'homme même.* My style—how I behave—expresses what I am in my truest and deepest self. Out of the abundance of the heart the mouth speaks. Or perhaps Hopkins is more apposite:

> Selves—goes itself; *myself* it speaks and spells
> Crying *What I do is me; for that I came.*[64]

This means that Vatican II, the "pastoral council," has a teaching, a "doctrine" that to a large extent it has been difficult for us to formulate because in this case doctrine and spirit are two sides of the same coin. Cardinal Ottaviani was correct when he insisted in the council that pastoral could not be separated from doctrinal.[65] The council taught a number of things. Among them is a teaching on the style of the Church. It did not "define" that teaching but taught it on almost every page through the form it adopted. Moreover, this teaching on the style of the Church was an implicit but insistent call for a change in style—a style less autocratic and more collaborative, a style willing to listen to different viewpoints and take them into account, a style open-and-above board, a style less unilateral in its decision-making, a style committed to fair play and to working with persons and institutions outside the Catholic community, a style that assumes innocence until guilt is proven, a style that eschews secret oaths, anonymous denunciations, and inquisitorial tactics. This is the style for the Church that Pope John seemed to be pointing toward in his allocution on October 11, 1962, opening the Second Vatican Council: the Church should act by "making use of the medicine of mercy rather than severity . . . and by showing herself to be the loving mother of all, benign, patient, full of mercy and goodness."[66]

The shift of Vatican II in style of discourse has, therefore, deep ramifications. It and the many other special features I have mentioned distinguish this council from every previous one. By adopting the style it did Vatican II redefined what a council is. Vatican II, that is to say, did not take the Roman senate as its implicit model. I find it difficult to pinpoint just what its implicit model was, but it seems much closer to guide, partner, friend, and inspired help-mate than it does to lawmaker, police officer, or judge.

Interpreting the Council

How do we interpret Vatican II? That is the problem that has beset us for 40 years. One reason we have been so frustrated has been the lack of a hermeneutic that would take style into account. Proof-texting has a bad name, but I think that, if it can work anywhere, it can work in the interpretation of the councils up to Vatican II, because most of their conciliar pronouncements were discrete units. My impression is that interpreters of Vatican II have often been applying a form of proof-texting to advance their positions, quoting a line here or a passage there but without taking account of the genre. This cannot work for Vatican II. Content gets divorced from form and the "letter" divorced from the "spirit."

It was precisely to forestall such an outcome that the synod of 1985 laid down its norms. Those norms asked us to look at the council in its totality and to recognize its coherence and integrity. I believe that by approaching the documents of the council through their form and vocabulary, as well as through their "content," we have the basis for a method that can fulfill those norms and accomplish the ideal the synod proposed:[67]

(1) Each passage and document of the council must be interpreted in the context of all the others, so that the integral teaching of the council can be rightly grasped.

(2) The four constitutions of the council (liturgy, Church, revelation, and Church in the modern world) are the hermeneutical key to the other documents—namely, the council's nine decrees and three declarations.

(3) The pastoral import of the documents ought not to be separated from, or set in opposition to, their doctrinal content.

(4) No opposition may be made between the spirit of the council and the letter of the council.

(5) The council must be interpreted in continuity with the great tradition of the Church, including other councils.

(6) Vatican II should be accepted as illuminating the problems of our day.

As they stand, these norms could hardly be improved upon. They need to be complemented by a seventh norm that takes account of discontinuity. Yes, Vatican II affirmed again and again its continuity with the Catholic tradition, especially with the councils of Trent and Vatican I. That is incontestable. Vatican II changed nothing in what Cardinal Dulles calls its "substantive teaching." Moreover, it did nothing that in any way diminished the authority structures in the Church. "Servant leaders" know the buck stops with them, as the council insisted. Nonetheless, the questions recur: Is there a "before" and an "after" Vatican II? Is there any noteworthy discontinuity between the council and what preceded it? Did anything happen? When the council ended in 1965, some 40 years ago, practically everybody would have answered those questions with a resounding affirmative, to the point that, as mentioned, Archbishop Lefebvre condemned the council as heretical and led a group into schism. Today, however, there are learned, thoughtful, and well-informed people who are responding in the negative. I could not be more in agreement with their affirmation of the profound continuity of the council with the Catholic tradition, an agreement it seems one can never repeat too often. As a historian, however, I believe that we must balance the picture by paying due attention to the discontinuities. When we do so, one thing at least becomes clear: the council *wanted* something to happen.

Notes

1. Agostino Marchetto, *Il Concilio ecumenico Vaticano II: Contrappunto per la sua storia* (Vatican City: Libreria Editrice Vaticana, 2005).
2. I take my information about the presentation from Sandro Magister, "Vatican II: The Real Untold Story," http:// chiesa.espresso.repubblica.it/articolo/34283&eng=y (accessed September 17, 2007). Sandro Magister is a journalist with the Italian periodical *L'Espresso*.
3. Giuseppe Alberigo and Joseph A. Komonchak, eds., *History of Vatican II*, 5 vols. (Maryknoll, N.Y.: Orbis, 1995–2005).
4. See Magister, "Vatican II" 1 (quoting Ruini) and Marchetto, *Concilio ecumenico Vaticano II* 378–79.
5. For an elucidation of the category, see Joseph A. Komonchak, "Vatican II as 'Event,'" republished in this volume. See also Maria Teresa Fattori and Alberto Melloni, ed., *L'Evento e le decisioni: Studi sulle dinamiche del concilio Vaticano II* (Bologna: Il Mulino, 1997).
6. Quoted by Magister, "Vatican II" (my translation).
7. See Cardinal Joseph Ratzinger, with Vittorio Messori, *The Ratzinger Report: An Exclusive Interview on the State of the Church*, trans. Salvator Attanasio and Graham Harrison (San Francisco: Ignatius, 1985) 35.

8. See, e.g., Cardinal Leo Scheffczyk, *La Chiesa: Aspetti della crisi postconciliare e corretta interpretazione del Vaticano II* (Milan: Jaca, 1998); Cardinal Avery Dulles, "Vatican II: The Myth and the Reality," *America* 188 (February 24, 2003) 7–11, and "Vatican II: Substantive Teaching," ibid. (March 31, 2003) 14–17; Edward Oakes, "Was Vatican II a Liberal or a Conservative Council?" *Chicago Studies* 41 (2004) 191–211.

9. See Magister, "Vatican II" 2 (quoting Ruini) and Marchetto, *Concilio ecumenico Vaticano II* 380.

10. "The Final Report: Synod of Bishops," *Origins* 15 (December 19,1985) 444–50, at 445–46.

11. *Acta synodalia sacrosancti concilii oecumenici Vaticani II,* 5 vols. (Vatican City: Typis polyglottis Vaticanis, 1970–1978) l:part 4, 647.

12. See, e.g., my *Trent and All That: Renaming Catholicism in the Early Modern Period* (Cambridge, Mass.: Harvard University, 2000) 10–11.

13. Gottfried Maron, "Das Schicksal der katholischen Reform im 16. Jahrhundert: Zur Frage nach der Kontinuität in der Kirchengeschichte," *Zeitschrift für Kirchengeschichte* 88 (1977) 218–29. See also Paolo Simoncelli, "Inquisizione romana e riforma in Italia," *Rivista Storica Italiana* 100 (1988) 5–125.

14. "Responsa ad epistolam circularem cancellarii Bismarck," in *Enchiridion symbolorum, definitionum et declarationum de rebus fidei et morum,* ed. Henricus Denzinger, Adolfus Schönmetzer, 33rd ed. (New York: Herder, 1965) nos. 3112–17, at no. 3116

15. See Peter Burke, *The French Historical Revolution: The Annales School 1929–89* (Stanford, Calif.: Stanford University, 1990).

16. See R. G. Collingwood, *The Idea of History* (New York: Oxford University, 1956) 42–45.

17. John Courtney Murray, "This Matter of Religious Freedom," *America* 112 (January 9, 1965) 43 (his emphasis).

18. *Acta synodalia* 1:part 1, 168, and also 171–72.

19. *Decrees of the Ecumenical Councils,* ed. Giuseppe Alberigo and Norman Tanner, 2 vols. (Washington: Georgetown University,

1990) 1:257. For a description of different uses of history in councils, see my "Reform, Historical Consciousness, and Vatican II's Aggiornamento," *Theological Studies* 32 (1971) 573–601, at 577–84.

20. Mansi, *Sacrorum conciliorum collectio* 32.669: "... homines per sacra immutari fas est, non sacra per homines." See my *Giles of Viterbo on Church and Reform: A Study in Renaissance Thought* (Leiden: Brill, 1968) 179–91. See also Bernard J. F. Lonergan, "*Exitenz* and *Aggiornamento*," in *Collection*, ed. Frederick E. Crowe and Robert M. Doran, Collected Works, vol. 4 (Toronto: University of Toronto, 1988) 222–31.

21. See Stephen Schloesser, *Jazz Age Catholicism: Mystic Modernism in Postwar Paris, 1919–1933* (Toronto: University of Toronto, 2005) 160–70.

22. The quantity of literature on this issue is overwhelming. Brian Tierney's little book, *The Crisis of Church and State, 1050–1300* (Englewood Cliffs, N.J.: Prentice-Hall, 1964) can still be profitably consulted. Among more recent studies especially commendable are Uta-Renate Blumenthal, *Church and Monarchy from the Ninth to the Twelfth Century* (Philadelphia: University of Pennsylvania, 1988), and H. E. J. Cowdrey, *Pope Gregory VII, 1073–1085* (New York: Oxford University, 1998).

23. See Brian Daley, "The *Nouvelle Théologie* and the Patristic Revival: Sources, Symbols, and the Science of Theology," *International Journal of Systematic Theology* 7 (2005) 362–82. See also my "Developments, Reforms, and Two Great Reformations: Towards a Historical Assessment of Vatican II," *Theological Studies* 44 (1983) 373–406.

24. Pius XII, "Humani generis," in *The Papal Encyclicals*, ed. Claudia Carlen, 5 vols. (New York: McGrath, 1981) 4:175–83, at 177.

25. See, e.g., Thomas O'Meara, "'Raid on the Dominicans': The Repression of 1954," *America* 170 (February 5, 1994) 8–16.

26. See Daley, "*Nouvelle*" 371–76.

27. See, e.g., Bernard J. F. Lonergan, "The Transition from a Classicist World View to Historical Mindedness," in *A Second Col-*

lection: Papers, ed. William F. J. Ryan and Bernard J. Tyrrell (Toronto: University of Toronto, 1996; orig. ed. 1974) 1–10.

28. See, e.g., the interesting intervention of Bishop Luigi Bettazzi in which he argued that collegiality was based on a long-standing theological and canonical tradition and that it was those who opposed it, not those who proposed it, who were the real *novatores* (*Acta synodalia* 2:part 2 484–87).

29. Pius XI, "Mortalium animos," in Carlen, *Encyclicals* 3:313–19, and Pius XII, "Humani generis," ibid. 4:175–83, at 176–77.

30. See, e.g., the widely used handbook by Heribert Jone, *Moral Theology*, trans. Urban Adelman, 15th ed. (Westminster, Md.: Newman, 1963) 70.

31. See, e.g., Gigliola Fragnito, *La Bibbia al rogo: La censura ecclesiastica e i volgarizzamenti della Scrittura, 1471–1605* (Bologna: Il Mulino, 1997).

32. See, e.g., Pius IX, "Syllabus," in Denzinger, *Enchiridion* nos. 2901–80, at no. 2955; Leo XIII, "Au milieu," in Carlen, *Encyclicals* 2:278–83, at 282, and Pius X, "Vehementer nos," ibid. 3:45–51, at 46: "The Roman Pontiffs have never ceased, as circumstances required, to condemn the doctrine of the separation of church and state." For an account of Murray's saga, see Donald E. Pelotte, *John Courtney Murray: Theologian in Conflict* (New York: Paulist, 1975) 27–73.

33. See Francis Dvornik, "Emperors, Popes, and General Councils," *Dumbarton Oaks Papers* 6 (1951) 3–23, and his *Early Christian and Byzantine Political Philosophy: Origins and Background*, 2 vols. (Washington: Dumbarton Oaks Center for Byzantine Studies, 1966). Although Dvonik made a few mistakes in fact, his basic point that the Roman Senate was the model for how councils operated is generally accepted. For a detailed treatment of pre-Nicaean councils, see Joseph Anton Fischer and Adolf Lumpe, *Die Synoden von den Anfängen bis zum Vorabend des Nicaenums* (Paderborn: Ferdinand Schöningh, 1997); Leo Donald Davis, *The First Seven Ecumenical Councils (325–787): Their History and Theology* (Collegeville: Liturgical, 1990; orig. ed. 1983); Fergus Millar, *The Emperor in the Roman World (31*

B.C.–A.D. 337) (Ithaca: Cornell University, 1977) 590–607; Richard J. A. Talbert, *The Senate of Imperial Rome* (Princeton: Princeton University, 1984) 431–87.

34. Alberigo and Tanner, *Decrees* 1:6.
35. Ibid. 1:31.
36. See M. Lalmant, "Canon," *Dictionnaire de droit canonique,* 7 vols. (Paris: Letouzey, 1935–65) 2:1283–88.
37. Alberigo and Tanner, *Decrees* 1:336.
38. Ibid. 1:597.
39. Ibid. 1:411.
40. See my "The Council of Trent: Myths, Misunderstandings, and Misinformation," in *Spirit, Style, Story: Essays Honoring John W. Padberg, S.J.,* ed. Thomas M. Lucas (Chicago: Loyola, 2002) 205–26.
41. On social disciplining and the Counter-Reformation, see my *Trent and All That* 114–16, with bibliography.
42. Gregory XVI, "Mirari vos," in Carlen, *Encyclicals* 1:235–40.
43. "De fontibus Revelationis," *Acta synodalia* 1:part 3, 14–26.
44. Ibid. 1:part 3, 27 (my translation).
45. Ibid. 1:part l, 309 (my translation).
46. See ibid. 1:part 3, 184–87, at 185.
47. Ibid. 1:part 4, 121 (my translation).
48. See ibid. 142–44.
49. See, e.g., George A. Kennedy, *Classical Rhetoric and Its Christian and Secular Tradition from Ancient to Modern Times* (Chapel Hill: University of North Carolina, 1980), and his *Greek Rhetoric under Christian Emperors* (Princeton: Princeton University, 1983).
50. John W. O'Malley, *Four Cultures of the West* (Cambridge, Mass.: Harvard University, 2004).
51. John W. O'Malley, *Praise and Blame in Renaissance Rome: Rhetoric, Doctrine, and Reform in the Sacred Orators of the Papal Court, c.1450–1521* (Durham, N.C.: Duke University, 1979).
52. See my introduction to *Spiritualia,* ed. John W. O'Malley, Collected Works of Erasmus, vol. 66, (Toronto: University of Toronto, 1988) ix–li, and especially my "Erasmus and

Vatican II: Interpreting the Council," in *Cristianesimo nella storia: Saggi in onore di Giuseppe Alberigo*, ed. Giuseppe Alberigo and Alberto Melloni (Bologna: Il Mulino, 1996) 195–211.

53. See, e.g., my "The Religious and Theological Culture of Michelangelo's Rome, 1508–1512," in Edgar Wind, *The Religious Symbolism of Michelangelo: The Sistine Ceiling*, ed. Elizabeth Sears (Oxford: Oxford University, 2000) xli–lii; Charles Trinkaus, *In Our Image and Likeness: Humanity and Divinity in Italian Humanist Thought*, 2 vols. (Chicago: University of Chicago , 1970); John M. McManamon, *Funeral Oratory and the Cultural Ideals of Italian Humanism* (Chapel Hill: University of North Carolina, 1989), and his *Pierpaolo Vergerio the Elder and Saint Jerome: An Edition and Translation of Sermones pro Sancto Hieronymo* (Tempe: Arizona Center for Medieval and Renaissance Studies, 1999).

54. Daley, "*Nouvelle*" 369.

55. Henri de Lubac, *The Splendour of the Church*, trans. Michael Mason (New York: Sheed & Ward, 1956; French original: Paris: Aubier, 1954).

56. *Acta synodalia* 5:part 1, 159: "Adhibetur genus litterarium concilio non conveniens."

57. See, e.g., Garry Wills, *Lincoln at Gettysburg: The Words that Remade America* (New York: Simon & Schuster, 1992).

58. See, e.g., Hubert Jedin and Giuseppe Alberigo, *La figura ideale del vescovo secondo la Riforma cattolica*, 2nd ed. (Brescia: Morcelliana, 1985).

59. *Gaudium et spes* no.1.

60. Ibid. no. 44.

61. Ibid. no. 37.

62. See, e.g., ibid. nos. 10–13; *Christus Dominus* no. 13; *Presbyterorum ordinis* no. 9.

63. *Gaudium et spes* no. 16.

64. Gerard Manley Hopkins, "As kingfishers catch fire," in *Gerard Manley Hopkins: The Major Works*, ed. Catherine Phillips, rev. ed. (Oxford: Oxford University, 2002) 129 (his italics).

65. See *Acta synodalia* 1:part 3, 27.

66. Ibid. 1:part 1, 166–75, at 172–73.

67. I am using Cardinal Avery Dulles's paraphrase in his "Vatican II: Myth" 9.

3.

AGAINST FORGETTING: MEMORY, HISTORY, VATICAN II

Stephen Schloesser, S.J.

The author argues that in the present discussion over the meaning of Vatican II, considered from the historical vantage point of 40 years, the council needs to be resituated as an event of the mid-20th century. Its break with the past, embodied in ruptures and reversals of long-standing Catholic mentalités, must be seen as a response to two world wars, the Holocaust, the Atomic Age, atheist Communism, postwar existentialism, and the Cold War. Current debates about whether "anything happened" at Vatican II should consider that the new age inaugurated by the council was not merely possible; it was morally necessary.

> *Under history, memory and forgetting.*
> *Under memory and forgetting, life.*
> *But writing a life is another story.*
> *Incompletion.*
> —Paul Ricoeur (1913–2005)[1]

FORTY YEARS AFTER ITS CONCLUSION, Vatican II is passing from memory into history. This transition is partly due to the
relentless cycles of human life: its eye-witness participants are passing away. It is also due to a historical rupture: the definitive passing
of an era—specifically, the passing of Communism and the Cold War
era, what François Furet called "the passing of an illusion."[2] The
council was largely framed by the traumatic events of 1956 and 1968:
the repression of popular uprisings by Russian tanks in Budapest
and Prague. Implicit in this Cold War tapestry were events that are
now largely unknown to a youthful generation precisely because they
are in the settled past:[3] Hitler's aggression and the Holocaust; the
Soviet empire whose seeds lay in the blood of Stalingrad; the Atomic
Age that was born at Hiroshima; the postwar division of the world
into two mutually exclusive ideologies and superpowers; and the
ever-present threat of nuclear annihilation. Opening as it did just
days before the darkest night of this epoch—the October Missile
Crisis of 1962—Vatican II occurred at a time when the world had to
endure its deepest anxieties. None of the players living in 1965 could
have foreseen that this nightmarish world would, quite suddenly and
unexpectedly, come to an end 25 years later. We who live in the 21st
century can now conclude with certainty, along with John Lewis
Gaddis, that "the world spent the last half of the 20th century having
its deepest anxieties not confirmed."[4]

John O'Malley's essay, "Vatican II: Did Anything Happen?"
opens with a wonderful vignette that shows us how much the council
is undergoing the process of memorialization. As living memories
(*milieux de mémoire*) pass over into memory sites (*lieux de
mémoire*), various constituents engage in a contest over whose
memories will become the monuments upon which future Catholic
self-understanding and identity will be based.[5] Looking at this
present-day contest with the eyes of a historian, I cannot help but
notice two things: First, how painfully obvious it is that the council
not only *did* break with the past, but, more importantly, just how
much—in the Cold War context—such a rupture was not only possible but *necessary*. Second, it becomes clear how much purposeful
forgetting—repression or amnesia—is required to make a case for
continuity. Ernest Renan's famous remark about the origins of

nations can be aptly applied here: "The essence of a nation is that all individuals have many things in common, and also that they have forgotten many things."[6]

O'Malley's basic insight about *how* the council, while keeping faith with tradition, also broke with the past struck me as a genuine revelation. I can now make sense of so much of that council's work that I could not without his hermeneutical key. And yet, seeing *how* the council did this has made me wonder only more insistently *why* such a rupture was not only conceivable but necessary. It was necessary precisely because of the council's historical location. The council occurred during the second half of the 20th century—a time when the world faced its deepest anxieties and had no idea whether or not they would soon be realized.

Content – Form – Context

John O'Malley has drawn on four decades of his thought about rhetorical genres—from *Giles of Viterbo on Church and Reform* (1968) through *Praise and Blame in Renaissance Rome* (1979) to *The First Jesuits* (1993) and *Four Cultures of the West* (2004)—to offer a profound insight into the revolutionary character of Vatican II. By investigating "a hermeneutic that would take style into account," O'Malley underscores the difference in style that distinguished Vatican II from "the 20 councils that preceded it." The council spoke in a retrieved humanistic genre: "It engaged in panegyric, in the *ars laudandi*, whose technical name is 'epideictic'."[7]

The epideictic oration is "a rhetoric of praise and congratulation" meant to "heighten appreciation for a person, an event, an institution, and to excite to emulation of an ideal." In holding up ideals, the documents of Vatican II "excite us to wonder and admiration." This entails focusing attention on the "big issues"—"the major doctrines of creation, redemption, sanctification." Keeping one's eyes on cosmic concerns leads to a kind of "magnanimity": the reader is invited "to rise above all pettiness and to strive for an expansive vision and a generous spirit." In contrast to medieval and Scholastic forms that aimed at defining concepts and proving points, the classical oration sought "to touch hearts and move hearers to action for their fellow human beings."[8]

By laying out this new hermeneutic that reveals the true nature of the council, O'Malley shows us *how* the council broke with the past. In shifting our focus "from content to form," O'Malley shows us *how* "the word that was received from the mouth of Christ and the Apostles" was handed on—without adulteration or change—in a genre adapted to listeners for whom customary rhetoric obscured the message. He does this to counter postconciliar attempts, beginning in the 1980s and continuing into the present, to insist that the council entailed no break or rupture with the past, no "before" and no "after"—in the anticipatory words of Pope John XXIII, no "new Pentecost."[9]

Paying attention to *form* and laying out *how* the council's pronouncements broke with the past helps avoid the deadlocks that seem to have come from competing interpretations of conciliar *content*. A focus on genre moves the discussion and discussants to a calmer place—and in these days of bitter opposition, this much-needed innovation merits both praise and gratitude.

However, it has the potential problem of letting us forget a crucial fact about the council: namely, that it retrieved the "big issues" and broke radically with the past for deeply historical and fundamentally anxious reasons. Certainly, it represented for many of its participants the "'end of the Counter-Reformation' or even 'the end of the Constantinian era.'"[10] But such evocations of the ancient past blind us to the most important fact about the Vatican Council: *it was a council of the mid-20th century*, the bloodiest of all centuries.[11] By taking Vatican II out of the mid-20th century, the questions that have become obsessive for some in our own day—"*Does* doctrine develop? *Can* the Church change?"—become footballs in an intramural game. But when we return the council to its context, we see that the question and answer are both more obvious: yes, the Church radically changed, and it did so for an important reason. In the post-1945 world it had an ethical imperative to do so.

Now that the council's participants have largely passed away and the event is passing from memory into history, we can see what they could not: the council was a response to cataclysmic shifts in the mid-20th century. It is precisely because those shifts were so enormous—consequences of the Jewish Holocaust, of a global war that claimed between 50 and 60 million lives, of the invention of the atomic bomb and the possibility of human annihilation, of the Cold War and the Soviet totalitarian empire, of decolonization and the end of Western hegemony—that the council needed to go back to the big issues and revisit fundamental questions. In such a world as this, What or who is God? What or who is the human person? What is the point of human existence? What is salvation? If salvation is available to those outside the Church, what is the Church? What is its role in history? Cosmic questions like these required a genre that was proportionate to their scope: the epideictic oration.

It is important to investigate *how* the council employed this genre. But it also seems important to survey *why* the council—in the years 1962 to 1965, framed by 1956 to 1968—needed to use such language. O'Malley has shifted our focus from *what* to *how*, from *content* to *form*. I would like to draw our attention from *form* to *context*—from *how* to *why*. Situating the council historically can illuminate its deeply anxious concerns, its need to respond humanistically to the fragmentation of the world as well as to the brutal inhumanity its participants had eye-witnessed. Seen against this horizon, the council's rupture with the past appears not only as a historical possibility. It seems to have been an ethical necessity.

Context: Fragmentary Filings Drawn to Magnets

It is striking to read the anxiety implicit in the council's major documents over the fact of human *fragmentation* and *disunity*. Why do I say that the anxiety is implicit? Because the council makes a claim over and over again about how the human race is becoming "unified"—a claim that is central to all that will follow. However, this claim was not so much a factual description as it was wishful thinking. If it is a commonplace that we speak with greater frequency and insistence about what we cannot control and hence fill us with anxiety,[12] we should pay attention to how frequently the council invokes the notion of a human race that is becoming increasingly "unified."

"The condition of the modern world," *Lumen gentium* declared in November 1964, was that "men of the present day are drawn ever more closely together by social, technical, and cultural bonds" (no. 1). "In this age of ours," began *Nostra aetate* in October 1965, "men are drawing more closely together and the bonds of friendship between different peoples are being strengthened" (no. 1). "It is clear that with the passage of time all nations are coming into a closer unity," concluded *Dignitatis humanae* in December 1965; "men of different cultures and religions are being bound together by closer links" (no. 15). *Gaudium et spes*, also promulgated in December 1965, invoked the authority of *Lumen gentium*: "the human race today is tending more and more towards civil, economic, and social unity" (no. 43; citing *Lumen gentium* no. 28). The council's self-understanding rested on its reading of the world as an entity coming into an ever closer unity. Was this understanding true?

In a sense we can answer yes. Technological innovations in communication and transportation had been radically altering perceptions of space and time since around 1880, giving the impression of a shrinking world.[13] In 1912, the distress call sent by the wireless operator of the sinking *Titanic* was relayed along the Atlantic coast from Newfoundland to New York and then (via cable) to Europe. By early morning the whole world had heard of the disaster. "This was simultaneous drama on the high seas," notes Stephen Kern, "driven by steam power and choreographed by the magic of wireless telegraphy."[14] Such a shrinkage of time led to a shortening of the valuable delays that had once allowed for discussion, diplomacy, and the prevailing of cool heads. The French historian Pierre Granet, writing on the eve of World War II, attributed the outbreak of its predecessor to the telegraph: "The constant transmission of dispatches between governments and their agents, the rapid dissemination of controversial information among an already agitated public, hastened, if it did not actually provoke, the outbreak of hostilities."[15] This shrinkage in time would lead to an unprecedented and meaningless massacre, a correlative technological shrinkage of space having made possible a "movement of men and matériel on a scale never witnessed before in history."[16] The wartime loss of faith in progress was restored somewhat by Charles Lindbergh's flight in

1927 compressing the perceived distance of the Atlantic. The crowds that greeted him seemed "as if all the hands in the world [were] touching or trying to touch the new Christ and that the new Cross [was] the Plane."[17] Thirty years later, this shrinkage of both space and time multiplied geometrically after the Soviet Union's successful launch of the first intercontinental ballistic missile in August 1957 and the orbit of *Sputnik* two months later. Nuclear warheads could now reach the United States in half an hour.[18] Thus, by 1962, although altered perceptions of space and time led to a shrinking world, this contributed less to global "unity" than to an exponentially increased global anxiety.

In another sense, then, we can answer no: the council's claim for global "unity" was frighteningly—and obviously—false. The world had become, if anything, so deeply fragmented that the situation seemed both necessary and unalterable. This global fracturing was a result of the end of European hegemony in the West in two different yet related aspects.

The first aspect was the Cold War. European domination of the world came to a definitive end in 1945. Out of its ashes emerged two much younger superpowers, former allies who quickly became enemies. On March 5, 1946, Winston Churchill would declare in Fulton, Missouri, that "an iron curtain has descended across the Continent."[19] One year later, Charles Bohlen could write, "Instead of unity among the great powers—both political and economic—after the war, there is complete disunity between the Soviet Union and the satellites on one side and the rest of the world on the other. There are, in short, two worlds instead of one."[20]

Out of this fundamental disunity events quickly cascaded. From June 1948 to September 1949, America's Berlin Airlift countered the Soviet attempt to starve out the isolated Western zone. The formation of the Federal Republic of Germany in May 1949 gave a geographical foothold for the Marshall Plan to counter Soviet expansion. That same year also witnessed the USSR's detonation of its first atomic weapon marking an end to the USA's nuclear monopoly, as well as Mao Zedong's communist victory in China. In 1950–1953, China's involvement in the Korean War forced a settlement without an American victory. In March 1954, the Americans tested a thermonuclear device that yielded 750 times that of the bomb dropped on Hiroshima. Soviet scientists issued their top-secret report on this event's significance: "The detonation of just a hundred hydrogen bombs could 'create on the whole globe conditions impossible for life.'"[21] In November 1956, Kruschev coupled the ruthless Soviet repression of the Hungarians' uprising with a threat against Britain and France to send "'rocket weapons' if they did not immediately withdraw their forces" from the Suez Canal. From 1957 through 1961, adds John Gaddis, "Kruschev openly, repeatedly, and bloodcurdlingly threatened the West with nuclear annihilation."[22] Fidel Castro's successful Cuban revolution on New Year's Day 1959, followed by the Bay of Pigs fiasco in April 1961, provided an opportunity for Soviet missiles to be located just off the coast of the U.S. mainland. The Berlin Wall, an act of desperation, was constructed four months later.

In short, the mutual escalation of nuclear anxiety not only accelerated quickly during the decade preceding the council, but it reached its most terrifying moment, curiously enough, during the very week following the council's opening (October 11, 1962). The "thirteen days" of the Cuban Missile Crisis—during which the world discovered what it meant to be only minutes from the nuclear annihilation of millions—took place from October 16 to 28. Surprisingly, Xavier Rynne's eyewitness account (published in installments in the *New Yorker*) made no mention of the crisis, focusing solely on the debate over Latin and the liturgy that took place during those days.[23] Henri Fesquet also did not mention the crisis directly, but inserted remarks on "The Council and the Atomic Bomb" in his entry for October 26, 1962. He included excerpts from a petition circulated by conciliar clergy and another circulated by Roman laity that quoted Cardinal Ottaviani: "All war must be prohibited. Those who see clearly that their government is making preparations for the carnage and ruin of the people by means of war can and should overthrow that regime by just means."[24]

With a perspective offered by 40 years' distance, Gerald Fogarty surveys both the Missile Crisis itself as well as Pope John XXIII's intervention in it, filling in gaps of memory with history.[25] On October 25, the pope gave an unscheduled noon speech broadcast in French and addressed to "all men of good will." The following day, the *New York Times* gave front-page coverage to the pope's words and published the speech in full. The same day, *Pravda* published an account of the speech ending with these words: "To agree to negotiations at any level and at any location to be well-inclined to these negotiations and to commence them—this would be a sign of wisdom and cautiousness that would be blessed by heaven and earth."[26] The pope's intervention inaugurated a period of mutual overtures between himself and Kruschev.

Six months after the Missile Crisis, John XXIII published his encyclical *Pacem in terris* (April 11, 1963). Echoing his speech during the October crisis, the encyclical departed from tradition and addressed itself "to all Men of Good Will."[27] When the pope died just a little over two months later (on June 3), "Soviet Navy ships in Genoa harbor flew their flags at half-mast. 'Good Pope John' had made his impact on the Communist world."[28] Five months later, the world witnessed the assassinations of both President Ngo Dinh Diem of South Vietnam (November 2) and President John F. Kennedy (November 22)—a pairing reminding us of the painful linkages between the Cold War and decolonization. The following year, two now-classic films about the threat of global nuclear annihilation hit the silver screen: Stanley Kubrick's dark comedy, *Dr. Strangelove or: How I Learned to Stop Worrying and Love the Bomb*; and Sidney Lumet's dead serious *Fail Safe*. One year later, Peter Watkins's *The War Game* (1965), a drama-documentary account of a nuclear attack, was judged by the British Broadcasting Corporation as "too horrifying for the medium of broadcasting." The decision not to show the film on national television set in motion a public uproar.[29]

If the Cold War between two superpowers was one aspect of the end of European hegemony in the West, a second aspect was the process of decolonization that ran roughly from 1945 to 1970. The process was a bitter one. Europeans had taken traditional units of identity and belonging—most notably clans and tribes—and artificially grouped them (some of them ancient enemies) into states. While there was no returning to the traditional world of the pre-nation-state, there was also no easy way to negotiate emergent identities in states internally composed of tribal and ethnic antagonists. Additionally, since decolonization happened to take place within the context of the Cold War, emergent states found themselves financially and politically pressured to align themselves with the "Free" world or the "Communist" world—or, in the case of more independent temperaments, to play the wild card of "non-alignment."[30]

The British granted India and Pakistan independence in 1947, inaugurating bloody Muslim–Hindu conflicts. Korean independence in 1945 and the establishment of the People's Republic of China in 1949 were quickly followed by the Korean conflict of 1950 to 1953, an attempt to limit Asian Communist expansion that drew in forces from the newly formed United Nations. As early as 1945, with the departure of defeated Japanese troops from occupied Indochina, Ho Chi Minh declared an independent state of Vietnam. A red scare caused the United States to reverse its wartime opposition to continued French colonialism and support imperialism rather than Vietnamese self-determination. The bloody fighting ended for the French in 1954 with the catastrophic defeat at Dien Bien Phu, but it was only beginning for the Americans after the partition of Vietnam into North and South. The state of Israel declared its independence in 1948 and was immediately invaded by Egypt, Lebanon, Iraq, and Syria. Israel won the ensuing war and consolidated its territory in the armistice of 1949. The Six Day War of 1967 would increase Israeli territory and affect geopolitics in the region to the present day.

Dates of declared national independence also show just how embedded Vatican II was in this unprecedented new world: 1945—Indonesia, Korea, Lebanon, Syria; 1946—Jordan, Philippines; 1947—Bengal, India, Pakistan; 1948—Burma, Israel; 1949—Indonesia; 1951—Libya; 1953—Cambodia, Korean War armistice; 1954—Laos, North and South Vietnam; 1956—Morocco, Sudan, Tunisia; 1957—Ghana, Malaya; 1958—Guinea; 1960—Cameroon, Central African Republic, Chad, Congo (Zaire), Cyprus, Dahomey (Benin), Gabon, Ivory Coast, Madagascar, Mali, Mauritania, Niger, Senegal, Somalia; 1961—Sierra Leone; 1962—Algeria, Burundi, Rwanda, Uganda; 1964—Kenya, Malawi, Tanzania, Zambia; 1965—Gambia, Rhodesia; 1966—Lesotho; 1967—Yemen; 1968—Botswana, Equatorial

Guinea, Swaziland. In the United States, as Malcolm X made explicit in his *Autobiography* (1965), African-American leaders imaginatively linked their own struggles for civil rights to the broader global movements.[31] Far from being a triumphant endpoint, Brown vs. Board (1954) turned out to be only the beginning of a long period of conflict that would include the Civil Rights Act (1964), race riots in Watts (1965–66), Detroit and Newark (1967), and the assassinations of Malcolm X (1965) and Martin Luther King, Jr. (1968).

In sum: far from growing together in "unity," the end of the colonial period meant that the world was fragmenting into many smaller entities. As Gaddis notes, the international system during the late 1950s, 1960s, and early 1970s "*appeared* to be one of bipolarity in which, like iron filings attracted by magnets, all power gravitated to Moscow and Washington." In fact, however, things were far more complicated than they looked, as the superpowers found it "increasingly difficult to manage the smaller powers. . . . The weak were discovering opportunities to confront the strong."[32]

As a corollary, Westerners now had to take the "Other" of the rest of the world seriously. Liberal imperialist ideology had been "Orientalist": Western representations of the "East" were not so much about what indigenous peoples were in themselves as the obverse of the West's self-imagination—"its contrasting image, idea, personality, experience."[33] In the Victorian age, new biological notions of "race" intersected with gendered cultural stereotypes to produce a linkage of male dominance with white supremacy: if the Westerner was civilized, adult, "manly," rational, sober, chaste, and hard-working, the Oriental was represented as being primitive (or "savage"), childlike, superstitious, feminine (or "effeminate"), debauched, promiscuous, and lazy.[34] Christian missionaries had been invaluable collaborators in the colonialist project albeit in far more complex ways than have previously been constructed.[35] In the postcolonial era, the imaginations of both former colonizers and colonized would have to be adjusted, constantly measuring their mutual projections against factual givens.

In 1962, when the council posed the question "What is the church?", this was the context: a Cold War division of the world into two mutually exclusive superpower ideologies; the bitter and bloody fragmentation of colonial possessions into multiple smaller nation-states, in conflict both within themselves as well as with other states; and a need to move beyond an Orientalist perspective. This would involve taking seriously other identities on their own terms, including religious (Islam, Hinduism, and Buddhism), nationalist (often artificially imposed), and ethnic (Indian, African, African-American). Contrary to the claims of the council, the idea of human unity was not a reflection of fact. It was instead a representation of deep hope for a world that seemed impossible in 1962–1965. This hope for unity in turn led to a magnanimous answer in reply to a very big question: "What is the church?"

Content: From the Domestic to the Global
or, What Is the Church?

"What is the church?" We know how the initial proposed schema, *De Ecclesia*, answered that question: the mystical body of Christ identified with the Roman Catholic Church; membership based on acknowledging the authority of the Roman pontiff; maximum extension of the infallible magisterium; ecumenical minimalism; and so on. The drafters of the schema seemed to have had endless concerns about "the question of authority," and the document itself "imagined a Church deeply disturbed by the crisis of authority: 'strongly shaken by deeply felt anguish (*vehementi afflictione percellitur*).'"[36] We also know that this schema was immediately rejected, the game having been lost even before *De Ecclesia* began to be discussed by the fathers.[37] The historical context tells us *why*: the answer was simply "not big enough." An anxious restatement of "authority" was inadequate to a situation in which Roman Catholicism, a largely Western European entity, had become just one in a multitude of competing new identities. The form tells us *how*: conciliar references to the Church were largely epideictic orations devoted to praise of this instrumental sign—sacrament—of the possibility of human unity.

Thus *Sacrosanctum concilium* (December 4, 1963) states, in the first sentence to be promulgated by the council, that it wants "to adapt more closely to the needs of our age those institutions which are subject to change; to foster whatever can promote *union* among all who believe in Christ" (no. 1). The liturgy is meant to "show forth the Church, a *sign* lifted up among the nations, to those who are outside, a *sign* under which the scattered children of God may be gathered together until there is *one* fold and *one* shepherd" (no. 2). The importance of the liturgy is its reconciling function: Christ's "humanity *united* with the Person of the Word was the instrument of our salvation. Therefore, 'in Christ the perfect achievement of our *reconciliation* came forth and the fullness of divine worship was given to us'" (no. 5).

This reconciliation would be a matter of unity but not linguistic-cultural uniformity. The first glimpses of Vatican openness to cultural adaptation had already appeared in December 1939 when the Sacred Congregation for Propagation of the Faith reversed Pope Clement XI's 150-year-old "perpetual" condemnation of the Jesuit Chinese Rites and did away with Benedict XIV's century-old oath. Such far-away concerns do seem, from this distance, to have been a strange preoccupation for Romans to have just three months after Hitler's September 1939 invasion of Poland and the outbreak of World War II. However, shortly after the end of World War I Pope Benedict XV had already begun the process of undoing his namesake's decision. This trend received even greater impetus with Japanese Imperial militarization and expansion throughout the 1930s: the Japanese invasion of Manchuria in 1931; the establishment of the puppet state of Manchukuo in 1932; the 1934 renunciation of the Washington Naval Conference; the 1936 abrogation of a commitment to disarmament; the 1937 invasion of China. "The destiny of the Church and the missions," writes George Minamiki, "was inextricably bound up with the momentous events that were taking place in the world."[38] Pius XII's 1939 revocation of earlier papal bans on Catholic veneration of ancestors and of Confucius can

be seen as a response to Chinese governmental statements supporting freedom of religion.

Although the particular case of missionary activity in China
would be radically altered after Mao Zedong's establishment of the
People's Republic of China in 1949, the broader principle of cultural
accommodation had already been established. Postwar decolonization catalyzed this radically new understanding of the Church's
relationship to the world. Instead of imposing a unitary ultramontanist culture, "inculturation" would be seen as the future imperative. While Latin was retained by the council as the language of
ecclesiastical identity, the vernacular was encouraged so that the one
unchanging word could be heard, preached, and appropriated in
many tongues. A new Pentecost had dawned. In *Sacrosanctum concilium*'s section laying out "Norms for Adapting the Liturgy to the
Temperament and Traditions of Peoples," the Church is described
as not wishing "to impose a rigid uniformity in matters which do
not involve the faith or the good of the whole community. Rather
does she respect and foster the qualities and talents of the various
races and nations" (no. 37). Unity replaced uniformity as the
guiding principle.

Lumen gentium, appearing one year later (November 21, 1964),
began its opening chapter, "The Mystery of the Church," by setting
forth the nature and mission of the Church—not in the anxious language of asserting *authority* (as the initially proposed schema had
done), but rather in an epideictic rhetoric appealing to the ideal end
of divine and human *unity*. The Church in the modern world,
declared *Lumen gentium*, is "in the nature of sacrament—a sign and
instrument, that is, of *communion* with God and of *unity* among all
men. . . . The condition of the modern world lends greater urgency
to this duty of the Church; for, while men of the present are drawn
ever more closely together by social, technical and cultural bonds, it
still remains for them to achieve *unity* in Christ" (no. 1). The "universal Church is seen to be 'a people brought into *unity* from the
unity of the Father, the Son and the Holy Spirit'" (no. 4). Through
the sacraments the faithful "are *united* in a hidden and real way to
Christ. . . . As all the members of the human body, though they are
many, form one body, so also are the faithful in Christ" (no. 7). The

college of bishops plays its role: "in so far as it is composed of many members, [it] is the expression of the multifariousness and universality of the People of God; and of the *unity* of the flock of Christ, in so far as it is assembled under one head" (no. 22). The Roman pontiff plays his role too, being "the perpetual and visible source and foundation of the *unity* both of the bishops and of the whole company of the faithful" (no. 23). These pastors in turn have the task of recognizing the laity's "contribution and charisms that everyone in his own way will, with one mind, cooperate in the common task" (no. 30). The laity "make the Church present and fruitful in those places and circumstances where it is only through them that she can become the salt of the earth" (no. 33). In sum, although "the sole Church of Christ . . . *subsists* in the Catholic Church, . . . many elements of sanctification and of truth are found *outside* its visible confines." These elements should be seen not as something alien but rather as "gifts belonging to the Church of Christ" and hence "forces impelling towards Catholic *unity*" (no. 8).

Gaudium et spes (December 7, 1965) further explored the way in which Christ is a "light to the nations." The Church "casts the reflected light of that divine life over all the earth" especially in the way "it *consolidates* society" (no. 40). "The *union* of the family of man is greatly consolidated and perfected by the *unity* which Christ established among the sons of God." "The encouragement of *unity* is in harmony with the deepest nature of the Church's mission. . . . It shows to the world that social and exterior *union* comes from a *union* of hearts and minds, from the faith and love by which its own indissoluble *unity* has been founded in the Holy Spirit." Since "the Church is *universal* in that it is not committed to any one culture or to any political, economic or social system," it "can be a very close bond between the various communities of men and nations," and so it calls upon all "to *consolidate* legitimate human organizations in themselves" (no. 42).

The Church can be this sign precisely because its members will remain united in faith even though they will disagree even in grave matters. The laity should realize that "their pastors will not always be so expert as to have a ready answer to every problem (even every grave problem) that arises; this is not the role of the clergy." It "happens rather frequently, and legitimately so, that some of the faithful, with no less sincerity," will see problems quite differently from one another. Thus, the laity should "try to guide each other by sincere *dialogue* in a spirit of *mutual charity*" with "anxious interest above all in the *common good*" and witness to Christ "at the very heart of the *community* of mankind" (no. 43). This final document of the council quotes *Lumen gentium*: "Since the human race is tending more and more towards civil, economic and social *unity*," priests are to "*unite* their efforts and combine their resources" under "the leadership of the bishops and the Supreme Pontiff and thus *eliminate division and dissension* in every shape and form, *so that* all mankind may be led into the *unity* of the family of God" (no. 43, quoting *Lumen gentium* no. 28).

Comparing these documents to the Church's vision of itself during its 200-year-old opposition to modernity and cultural adaptation demonstrates what a radical break they were with the past. In the earlier period, the Church was seen in an absolute binary opposition set over and against the "world." In the council the Church presented itself as a sacrament—both sign and instrument, transcendent and immanent, showing and effecting—an integrating *unity* that was promised and possible. In 1973, Archbishop (later Cardinal) Giovanni Benelli noted that there was "no doubt that in the Middle Ages and subsequently up to twenty years ago, there was in the Church a centralization of powers" that had "contributed to delaying for centuries the conversion of Asia." Recalling "the severity with which for so many years one had to observe the rules fixed by Rome" on ritual conformity, Benelli could only marvel: "And this, not some centuries ago but hardly twenty years ago."[39] The council had effected a postcolonialist sea change so deep that, a mere two decades later, it had become impossible to imagine what had existed before.

Context: "The Jewish Question"

Nostra aetate, the Declaration on the Relation of the Church to Non-Christian Religions, promulgated toward the end of the council (October 28, 1965), was primarily intended as a statement about the Jews. Read from the context of 1939 to 1945, it was intended to be a response to anti-Semitism throughout the ages and to the Holocaust in particular. As it was written within the 1960s context of Israeli-Palestinian strife, however, it needed to include a statement about Islam as well. In the end, it also briefly took account of Hinduism and Buddhism. As a result, by taking the "big questions" of religion as its starting point, this brief document curiously became a revolutionary one. It posed the question "What is religion?" in the broadest manner possible and affirmed truth and holiness in all places. This magnanimity made the Church's earlier stances—opposition to Eastern Orthodoxy and Protestantism, not to mention non-Christian religions—seem very small by contrast.

With the publication of *Nostra aetate,* the Church and the papacy had finally come to terms with modernity. Politically, Jewish emancipation had been one of the most significant markers of modernity, originating in Enlightenment thought and carried on in bourgeois Liberalism.[40] Eighteenth-century popes vacillated on the Jewish question. In 1769, Pope Clement XIV relaxed some of the restrictions on Jews and reassigned control over Rome's Jewish ghetto from the Holy Office of the Inquisition to the city's cardinal vicar. In 1775, Clement's successor, Pope Pius VI, reversed his predecessor's measures immediately after his election and instituted draconian ones: he rescinded all of the Jews' previous privileges, set up ghettoes in all the towns of the Papal States, forbade Jews to "speak familiarly" to Christians, and reintroduced a 16th-century papal provision requiring Jews to wear a special badge that identified them.[41] In France, Abbé Grégoire, a lower-clergy revolutionary thinker, argued for Jewish assimilation.[42] (Even then, however, it must be acknowledged that Grégoire referred to Jews as "parasitic plants who eat away the substance of the tree to which they are attached."[43]) Napoleon Bonaparte exported and implemented French revolutionary ideals across Europe, including his abolition of the papal ghetto and emancipation of the Jews in the 1809 occupation of Rome and exile of Pope Pius VII. After concluding a pact with the pope, Napoleon's legal reforms throughout occupied Europe met resistance: the "prospect of full Jewish emancipation raised by the Concordat was deeply—often violently—unpopular almost everywhere." Occupying French officials had outlawed the reading of liturgical texts blaming Jews for the death of Christ, and they "dreaded Easter all over the Empire." Throughout Holy Week in 1808, French troops were called in to quell the violent reactions of Catholic faithful in Pisa.[44]

After Napoleon's defeat, the Roman Republic was abolished and the Papal States were restored. Pope Pius VII, overly influenced by "the near-universal urgings of the cardinals around him," sent the Jews back into the ghettoes.[45] Papal opposition to Jewish emancipation—firmly reiterated by Pope Pius IX after French troops restored his throne following the 1848 revolution—became a salient symbol of ultramontanist Catholicism's refusal to accommodate modernity. The mid-century affair of Edgardo Mortara in 1858 became a *cause célèbre* for the free press throughout Europe and the United States; in reaction, various Catholic publications fostered an extreme anti-Semitism, the most important being the Jesuits' *Civiltà Cattolica*.[46] The symbolism of a Jewish boy's clandestine baptism, consequent abduction, and later adoption by his new "father," Pius IX—who three years later would declare himself unable to be reconciled with "progress, liberalism, and modern civilization"—was shot through with potential for dramatic depictions. The "Jewish Question" in the Papal States was resolved only in 1870 when Italian nationalists conquered Rome and put an end to papal territorial sovereignty. The Jews were freed from their ghettoes, and the pope became a self-imposed "prisoner of the Vatican."[47]

The "Jewish Question" as a metaphor for modernity famously erupted in France during the Dreyfus Affair (1894–1899).[48] Integralist French Catholics, who boasted that "the Church and the pope are one," had never shown much enthusiasm for Pope Leo XIII, and they ignored his appeal (in *Au milieu des sollicitudes* [February 16, 1892]) to "rally to the Republic."[49] Instead, the Assumptionists waged a vicious anti-Semitic campaign by means of their daily newspaper, *La Croix* (The Cross), and their magazine from Lourdes, *Le Pèlerin* (The Pilgrim).[50] (In 1998, *La Croix* finally apologized for its anti-Semitic editorials on the 100th anniversary of Émile Zola's open letter "J'accuse!" to the Republic's President.)[51] After Dreyfus's pardon (1899), radical (i.e., anti-clerical) governments were voted into power as a backlash against the anti-Dreyfusard forces of the Church and the Army.[52] A series of legislative acts (1901–1905) were passed leading to the expulsion of nearly all members of religious orders in France. After the Act of Separation of Church and State (1905), Rome overruled the French hierarchy and the recently installed Pope Pius X excommunicated all the legislators who had voted for separation laws. This political bumbling, reinforcing Catholic opposition to democratic government and implying support of the anti-Dreyfusard (and, hence, anti-Semitic) camp, led to a drastic decline in Catholic practice.[53]

In sum, Jewish rights and Catholic opposition to them had been a boundary marker of modernity since at least the mid-18th century. Theologically speaking, the Church opposed political emancipation for fear that this would lead to religious "indifferentism"—a forerunner of present-day fears about "relativism." Anthropologically, one could offer another interpretation: Jews were frightening precisely because they represented ambiguous—and thus dangerous— margins between the Christian self and its "Other."[54] Protestants, for all their differences, were still identifiably part of the Christian self. Conversely, Muslims represented the Orientalist "Other" of both Christianity and the geographical "West." Jews, however, resided in liminal margins—they were the ancestors of Christianity, they resided within the West, and they even resided within city walls. For centuries, then, they were kept in ghettos, persecuted, and frequently killed as a way of consolidating Christian identity.

For these political, theological, and anthropological reasons, the attempt to formulate a positive statement of Jewish identity with respect to Catholicism—even after seeing the horror of the Holocaust—turned out to be a complicated task. *Nostra aetate*'s tortured genesis suggests just how radical a rupture it posed.[55] In the late 1940s and throughout the 1950s, efforts were underway to effect some kind of Catholic-Jewish reconciliation.[56] Gertrud Luckner, having risked her life to save Jews and having survived the Ravensbrück concentration camp, worked tirelessly with her Freiburg circle to obtain official renunciations of anti-Semitism. An initial success with the German bishops was followed by disappointment. Cardinal Josef Frings (of Cologne) opposed Luckner's work and, in 1950 (the same year as Pius XII's *Humani generis*), a Vatican *monitum* warned against the indifferentism that could result from Christian-Jewish dialogue. The Holy Office also sent the Jesuits Augustin Bea, Robert Leiber, and Charles Boyer to investigate the Freiburg circle. A 1952 letter from Frings to the German bishops reiterated the earlier warning. Not until after the death of Pius XII did the German bishops—beginning in 1959—speak out about the Holocaust. However, in a wonderful irony of history, the Freiburg circle had already, by the mid-1950s, "won the support of the very people who had been sent by Pope Pius to investigate their work"— namely, Boyer, Leiber, and, most importantly, Bea.[57]

Other collaborating Catholics included Jacques Maritain, president of the International Council of Christians and Jews, whose efforts on behalf of Jewish civil rights extended back as far as his student days at the Sorbonne. A young Socialist raised in a free-thinking Protestant household, Maritain had been passing out pamphlets in support of Russian Jews when he met his future wife, Raïssa Oumançoff. After yet another deadly pogrom against Jews in Russia, Oumançoff had been brought to France by her parents so that she, as a female, might be able to receive an education. The Maritains knew what it was to be vilified: relationships with their right-wing cohorts (like the Thomist scholar Fr. Reginald Gariggou-Lagrange and the novelist Georges Bernanos), entered into after their conversions to Catholicism, grew increasingly sour throughout the menacing decade of the 1930s. In 1938, the Fascist journal *Je suis partout* attacked Maritain: "Jacques Maritain married a Jew. He has jewified (*enjuivé*) his life and his doctrine. His theology, his dialectic are falsfied like the passport of a Jewish spy." Fortunately the Maritains found exile in New York City. Their friend Max Jacob—"Jewish by race, Breton by birth, Roman by religion, sodomite by custom," eulogized the now-collaborationist *Je suis partout*—was not so fortunate, dying in the Drancy transit as he awaited the convoy for

Auschwitz. Raïssa Maritain recorded the death: "Max gave his life with the humility of a saint." Jacques concurred: "Max Jacob died a saint."[58]

Already in 1946 Maritain had written Msgr. Giovanni Battista Montini (later Pope Paul VI) saying that "what Jews and also Christians need above all (at this juncture) is a voice—the paternal voice, the voice par excellence, that of the vicar of Jesus Christ—to tell the truth to the world and shed light on this tragedy"—that is, "six million Jews have been *liquidated*."[59] As France's ambassador to the Holy See, Maritain "pressed Rome emphatically to take the lead in condemning the Holocaust atrocities and European anti-semitism." Frustrated "when he saw that his efforts were to no avail," Maritain resigned his post.[60]

Pius XII died in 1958 and was succeeded by Angelo Roncalli who, as apostolic delegate to Turkey during the Holocaust, "saved a number of Croatian, Bulgarian and Hungarian Jews by assisting their emigration to Palestine."[61] In December 1959, one year after assuming the papacy as John XXIII, Roncalli made Augustin Bea a cardinal and installed him as president of the Pontifical Council for Promoting Christian Unity. (Bea was ordained a bishop two years later.) Although *Nostra aetate*'s final form was not as strong as Bea wanted—in the end it had neither an explicit apology for centuries of practice nor an explicit rejection of the word "deicide"—the pro-mulgation of this document was largely Bea's doing, and it reversed centuries of Catholic (including papal) anti-Semitism.[62] Ironically, in the final analysis, this innovative magisterial teaching was due primarily to the tireless efforts of lay persons—especially Luckner and Maritain—who would not let hierarchical intransigence over-come their personal experience of the horrors of 1939–1945.

Content: From Jewish Question to Cosmic Question or, What Is Religion?

The epideictic genre of *Nostra aetate* is evident from its first paragraph. It begins once again with a statement that represses the unacceptable truth: "Men are drawing more closely together and the bonds of friendship between different peoples are being strengthened." (This opening line, a now-familiar generic description of "this age of ours," seems somewhat strained, given the delicate political machinations involved in Pope Paul VI's journey to the Holy Land in January 1964—enthusiastically received by Muslims, including a warm reception by King Hussein of Jordan, and shown official courtesy by the state of Israel, a national entity not recognized by the Papal State.)[63] Then follows the fundamental orientation of the council's self-understanding: "Ever aware of her duty to foster *unity* and charity among individuals, and even among nations, she reflects at the outset on what men have in common and what tends to promote fellowship among them" (no. 1).

What do human beings have in common? They "look to their different religions for an answer to the unsolved riddles of human existence." This paragraph—which might as well be called "What is religion?"—is one of the most poignant in all the conciliar documents. In asking all the "big questions" of human existence, it challenges any reader to recover the widest possible horizons of perspective. "What is man? What is the meaning and purpose of life? What is upright behavior, and what is sinful? Where does suffering originate, and what end does it serve? How can genuine happiness be found? . . . And finally, what is the ultimate mystery, beyond human explanation, which embraces our entire existence, from which we take our origin and towards which we tend?" (no. 1). As I will suggest below, this profound list of perennial questions owes itself to the atheistic and existentialist context of the postwar era.

From here the council affirms Hinduism, Buddhism, and other religions that "attempt in their own ways to calm the hearts of men" (no. 2). Rejecting "nothing of what is true and holy in these religions," the Church urges Christians, "while witnessing to their own faith and way of life," to "acknowledge, preserve and encourage the spiritual and moral truths found among non-Christians, also their social life and culture" (no. 2). Here immediately follows this affirmation: "The Church has also a high regard for the Muslims" who "worship God, who is one, living and subsistent, merciful and almighty, the Creator of heaven and earth" (no. 3). Taken along with the affirmation of Hinduism and Buddhism, this is a long way from the words of Pius XI addressed to the Sacred Heart of Jesus published almost exactly 40 years earlier: "Be Thou King of all those who even now sit in the shadow of idolatry or Islam, and refuse not Thou to bring them into the light of Thy kingdom."[64] Without directly naming the Crusades—an enduring event of traumatic proportions for Arab self-identity—the declaration notes that over the centuries "many quarrels and dissensions have arisen between Christians and Muslims." It "now pleads with all to forget the past, and urges that a sincere effort be made to achieve mutual understanding" (no. 3). These words had been crafted with an eye to Arab-Israeli tensions—tensions that would explode two years later in the Six Day War of 1967.

Now the document turns to its primary intention, an aim of Cardinal Bea since his encounter with Gertrud Luckner and the Freiburg Circle: an attempt to deal with centuries of Christian anti-Semitism. First comes the verdict on whether Jews bear the burden of Christ's death: "Neither all Jews indiscriminately at that time, nor Jews today, can be charged with the crimes committed during his passion" (no. 4). Again, the contrast in tone with Pius XI's prayer of exactly 40 years earlier is striking: "Look, finally, with eyes of pity upon the children of that race, which was for so long a time Thy chosen people; and let Thy Blood, which was once invoked upon them in vengeance, now descend upon them also in a cleansing flood of redemption and eternal life."[65]

Next comes a directive instructing all to stop speaking of the Jews "as rejected or accursed as if this followed from holy Scripture." Whether "in catechizing or in preaching the Word of God," all are warned not to "teach anything which is not in accord with the truth of the Gospel message or the spirit of Christ." These instructions would eventually find their way into the Church's revised liturgy. The ancient Good Friday prayer for the "perfidious Jews" that had once been abolished throughout Europe by French revolutionary law enforced by Napoleon's troops would be replaced by a new prayer "for the Jewish people, the first to hear the word of God, that they may continue to grow in the love of his name and in faithfulness to his covenant."[66]

Finally comes the paragraph on the anti-Semitism of the past, delicately and diplomatically phrased so as to avoid giving offense to Arabs. Embedding its reproach within the wider frame of reproving "every form of persecution against whomsoever it may be directed," the text underscores that it is "moved not by any political consideration, but solely by the religious motivation of Christian charity" and a memory of the Church's "common heritage with the Jews." The final line is not an apology from below but rather a condemnation from above. It deplores "all hatreds, persecutions, displays of antisemitism leveled at any time or from any source against the Jews" (no. 4).

The history of *Nostra aetate* leads the reader into fascinating territory. It tells us something about how doctrine actually "develops"—that is, by means of little people who battled ecclesiastical authorities, whose cause won over those sent to investigate them (e.g., Augustin Bea), and whose legacy is no less important now that the world has largely forgotten them (e.g., Luckner and Maritain). And it tells us how the circles of bitterly entrenched positions were able to be squared by stepping back and asking much larger questions like the one that opened this declaration: "what is the ultimate mystery, beyond human explanation, which embraces our entire existence, from which we take our origin and towards which we tend?" (no. 1). In returning the reader to ultimate sources, epideictic rhetoric allows for a rethinking of the world and, if necessary, radical revisions. It is a literary genre with a sharp ethical edge.

Context: Liberty, Tolerance, and Totalitarianism

The Declaration on Religious Liberty does not begin but rather ends with the panegyric to *unity* seen in other documents: "It is clear that with the passage of time all nations are coming into a closer *unity*, men of different cultures and religions are being bound together by closer links, and there is a growing awareness of individual responsibility. Consequently, to establish and strengthen *peaceful relations* and *harmony* in the human race, religious freedom must be given effective constitutional protection everywhere and that highest of man's rights and duties—to lead a religious life with freedom in society—must be respected" (no. 15). Why the document did not begin with this motif is suggested by where it does begin: a searching "the sacred tradition and teaching of the Church, from which it draws forth new things that are always in harmony with the old" (no. 1). The teaching of this document was such a radical reversal of centuries of the Church's magisterium and practice that it began with addressing the fundamental anxiety provoked by such a rupture with the past. It needed first to try to establish that religious freedom was consonant with the past. This required some very complex gymnastics.

At least since Theodosius (d. 395) and the invention of "Christendom," the Church had stood against religious freedom, and it expressed this opposition in both practice and doctrine. Saint Augustine's famous employment of Christ's parable about the wedding banquet against the Donatists stood as the medieval source: "let the heretics and schismatics come from the highroads and hedges. *Compel them to come in.* . . . 'Let us come in of our own free will,' they say. That wasn't the order the Lord gave: *Compel them,* he said, *to come in.* Let necessity be experienced outwardly, and hence free willingness be born inwardly."[67] The use of torture to enforce social conformity (via religious confession) was commonplace in the Middle Ages and beyond.[68] Jews, Waldensians, Albigensians, and other "heretics" stood beside "witches," "lepers," and "sodomites" as medieval groups—whether official ones (like the medieval Inquistion) or popular mobs (sometimes restrained by ecclesiastical authorities)—produced a "persecuting society."[69] Torture and execution continued to be accepted as routine throughout the the 16th and 17th centuries as the newly confessional states, both Catholic and Protestant, enforced the modern aim of one ruler, one religion, one people.[70]

"Tolerance" was one of the battle cries of Enlightenment writers in France, especially demanding religious liberty for Protestants and political emancipation for Jews. Pope Pius VII's eventual concordat with Napoleon (July 15, 1801) did acquiesce in recognizing only "that the Catholic Apostolic and Roman religion is the religion of the great majority of French citizens."[71] But "enemies of the Enlightenment" throughout the 19th century fought the idea of toleration as leading to religious indifferentism.[72] Papal teaching repeatedly condemned the constitutional liberties spreading across Europe: liberties of the press, speech, religion, and (manhood) suffrage.

"This shameful font of indifferentism," wrote Gregory XVI, "gives rise to that absurd and erroneous proposition which claims that *liberty of conscience* must be maintained for everyone. It spreads ruin in sacred and civil affairs, though some repeat over and over again with the greatest impudence that some advantage accrues to religion from it. . . . Experience shows, even from earliest times, that cities renowned for wealth, dominion, and glory perished as a result of this single evil, namely immoderate freedom of opinion, license of free speech, and desire for novelty." From here Gregory went on to condemn "that harmful and never sufficiently denounced freedom to publish any writings whatever and disseminate them to the people, which some dare to demand and promote with so great a clamor."[73]

Pius IX reaffirmed the words of his predecessor: "From which totally false idea of social government they do not fear to foster that erroneous opinion, most fatal in its effects on the Catholic Church and the salvation of souls, called by Our Predecessor, Gregory XVI, *an insanity*, viz., that 'liberty of conscience and worship is each man's personal right, which ought to be legally proclaimed and asserted in every rightly constituted society; and that a right resides in the citizens to an absolute liberty, which should be restrained by no authority whether ecclesiastical or civil, whereby they may be able openly and publicly to manifest and declare any of their ideas whatever, either by word of mouth, by the press, or in any other way.'"[74] In addition, Pius explicitly condemned these propositions in the Syllabus of Errors:

> 15. Every man is free to embrace and profess that religion which, led by the light of true reason, he may have thought true.
> 77. In this our age it is no longer expedient that the Catholic religion should be treated as the only religion of the state, all other worships whatsoever being excluded.

79. For truly it is false that the civil liberty of all worships and the full power granted to all of openly and publicly declaring any opinions or thoughts whatever, conduces to more easily corrupting the morals and minds of peoples and propagating the plague of indifferentism.[75]

Leo XIII reaffirmed his predecessors: "Justice therefore forbids, and reason itself forbids, the State to be godless; or to adopt a line of action which would end in godlessness—namely, to treat the various religions (as they call them) alike, and to bestow upon them promiscuously equal rights and privileges."[76] However, faced with the political problems of Catholics in France's Third Republic and during Bismarck's *Kulturkampf*, Leo suggested that a certain measure of "tolerance" was permissible in certain circumstances: "while not conceding any right to anything save what is true and honest, she (the Catholic Church) does not forbid public authority to tolerate what is at variance with truth and justice, for the sake of avoiding some greater evil, or of obtaining or preserving some greater good."[77] As noted above, four years later Leo urged French Catholics—unsuccessfully—to "rally to the Republic," but his successor Pius X would excommunicate every French legislator who had voted for the French separation laws. This action accorded with his namesake's condemned proposition in the Syllabus (1864): "55. The Church should be separated from the state, and the state from the Church."[78]

Not until Pope Pius XII's Christmas Allocution of 1945 did papal teaching unequivocally embrace the value of democratic government.[79] In hindsight, concordats made with the Fascist governments of Italy (February 11, 1929) and Germany (July 20, 1933) had protected church interests to some extent—but at great cost. Looking ahead, the post-1945 world would be one with limited choices: democracy and totalitarianism. The pope chose democracy. "Within the confines of each particular nation as much as in the whole family of peoples," wrote the pontiff, "state totalitarianism is incompatible with a true and healthy democracy."[80]

The Declaration on Religious Liberty, promulgated just 20 years later, was so contentious precisely because it represented a repudiation of centuries of church practice and doctrine.[81] Cardinal Siri voiced his concern that, if the doctrine of toleration were changed, "we will be undermining theological and our own authority."[82] John Courtney Murray—whose Jesuit superiors had ordered him in 1955 to stop writing on church-state issues[83]—explicitly realized that his opponents feared "the affirmation of progress in doctrine that an affirmation of religious freedom necessarily entails."[84] In 1963, the historian Msgr. John Tracy Ellis—whose superiors had forbidden him to attend a European conference in 1955—recorded hearing Murray at a dinner talk voice the possibility "that Newman's idea of the evolution of dogma might well become one of the key ideas in Vatican Council II."[85] Perhaps of greatest importance was pressure exerted by bishops from behind the Iron Curtain. One "moment"—that is, the context of monarchies in which the Church had formulated its teaching and practice of "established religion"—was dead. A second "moment"—that is, freedom of the Church against atheistic Communism—presented unprecedented challenges, especially in Czechoslovakia, Poland, and Yugoslavia.[86] In order to construct a response adequate to such a historical upheaval, the declaration would need to return to big questions.

Content: Between Liberalism and Communism or, What Is the Human Person?

The opening line of the declaration reads: *Dignitatis humanae*, that is, "*Of the dignity of the human person* is contemporary man becoming increasingly conscious" (no. 1). Significantly, the council did not follow a line of reasoning from the Enlightenment tradition of Liberal individualism and human "rights." Rather, it chose language borrowed from the philosophy of "personalism"—an approach based on interpersonal duties and mutual obligations (as well as rights) that had been espoused during the interwar period by figures like Emmanuel Mounier and Max Scheler—to ground its understanding of the "person" being free from *coercion*. "The Vatican Council declares that the *human person* has a right to religious freedom. Freedom of this kind means that all men should be immune from *coercion* on the part of individuals, social groups and every human power." Consonant with Catholic tradition's appeal to both revealed and natural law, the council based this "right to religious freedom" on "the very *dignity of the human person* as known through the revealed word of God and by reason itself" (no. 2).

In this new world of totalitarian governments, freedoms traditionally negotiated for the Church by concordats were now derived from individual liberty. "The freedom or immunity from coercion in religious matters which is the right of individuals must also be accorded to men when they act in community. Religious communities are a requirement of the nature of man and of religion itself." This in turn entailed freedoms of assembly, speech, education, and the press: "Religious communities have the further right not to be prevented from publicly teaching and bearing witness to their beliefs by the spoken or written word. . . . Finally, rooted in the social nature of man and in the very nature of religion is the right of men, prompted by their own religious sense, freely to hold meetings or establish educational, cultural, charitable and social organizations" (no. 4).

This reversal of teaching applied to the family as well. One century earlier, in the case of Edgardo Mortara (1858), the Church had argued that the ancient patriarchal right of a father over his children (*puissance paternelle*)—vehemently defended by anti-Enlightenment thinkers[87]—was superceded by the right "acquired by the Church over the baptized infant," a right that was "of a superior and more noble order" than that of the parents. "In fact," asserted the Church's legal brief, "the Canonists and Theologians are in full agreement with this truth: that in no case should a baptized child be returned to infidel parents."[88] Those had been times shaped by monarchy. In these new times contextualized by Communism, however, the Church argued the opposite: "Every family, in that it is a society with its own basic rights, has the right freely to organize its own religious life in the home under the control of the parents. These have the right to decide in accordance with their own religious beliefs the form of religious upbringing which is to be given to their children" (no. 5).

Of all the "big questions" elicited by this radical document, the inviolability of human conscience stands out most boldly as a Cold War response to communist coercion. "It is through his conscience that man sees and recognizes the demands of the divine law. He is bound to follow this conscience faithfully in all his activity so that he may come to God, who is his last end. There he must not be forced to act contrary to his conscience" (no. 2). This claim was traced back through Scripture and tradition: "One of the key truths in Catholic teaching, a truth that is contained in the word of God and constantly preached by the Fathers, is that man's response to God by faith ought to be free, and that therefore nobody is to be forced to embrace the faith against his will" (no. 10). These words were supported by a footnote thick with references to Ambrose, Augustine, Gregory the Great, Clement III, and Innocent III. Christ himself was recalled as a master and Lord who "acted patiently in attracting and inviting his disciples. He supported and confirmed his preaching by miracles to arouse the faith of his hearers and give them assurance, but not to coerce them" (no. 11).

The document did acknowledge that members of the Church had not always acted in accordance with these ideals, but it drew a strong distinction between the actions of Christians and the teaching of the Church: "Although in the life of the people of God in its pilgrimage through the vicissitudes of human history there has at times appeared a form of behavior which was hardly in keeping with the spirit of the Gospel and was even opposed to it, it has always remained the teaching of the Church that no one is to be coerced into believing" (no. 12; no qualifying footnote was appended here). Today, especially in light of our painful awareness of coerced Christian "conversions" among indigenous peoples—including those in North America both during and after the colonial period[89]—this distinction can ring somewhat hollow. In 1965, however, ongoing decolonization had not yet led to the postcolonialist mentality that has become commonplace over the past 40 years.

Dignitatis humanae, one of the final fruits of the council, provides a miniature case study of Vatican II's break from the past in terms of content, form, and context. In terms of content, the document was as much or perhaps even more about the possibilities of doctrinal "development" as it was about religious liberty. In terms of form, it accomplished its task by drawing the reader away from an earlier rhetorical style—for example, vituperous condemnations of liberty as insanity—and redirecting attention to the most exalted possibilities of the human person's conscience and dignity.

However, the most significant aspect of the document was its context—it was championed by representatives from the two major blocks of the Cold War, and for each of them liberty of conscience and religion was a matter of ethical necessity. From the American side, *Dignitatis humanae* symbolized a long hoped-for vindication: church acceptance of the democratic pluralism that had been feared so long and condemned as the heresy of "Americanism" under the larger umbrella of "Modernism."[90] At Vatican II, the end of European domination in the world and the acceptance of Catholics within the United States (especially after the assassination of President Kennedy) allowed the American Catholic Church to come of age, achieving adulthood as a post-immigrant Church in a post-colonial world. Moreover, as the superpower of the free world, America's uniquely pluralistic religious history had to be taken seriously. Conversely, bishops speaking from within the Soviet bloc (like Karol Wojtyla) needed—and demanded—an unequivocal statement of an individual conscience's absolute inviolability from external coercion of any kind. In this sense, the "Constantinian church" truly had come to an end. Finding itself suddenly oppressed by a quasi-imperial regime with global reach and aspirations, the Catholic Church needed to accommodate itself accordingly. Cardinal Joseph-Léon Cardijn summed up the ethical imperative succinctly: "The Church cannot expect religious liberty when she is in a minority unless she practices it when she is in the majority."[91]

Context: The Challenge of Late-Modern Humanisms

Some of the most poignant passages in conciliar documents emanate from the Church's reversal of its long-standing dismissal of modernity in an attempt to take seriously the anxious concerns of contemporary humanity. Pius IX's Syllabus of Errors (December 8,

1864) had condemned the proposition that "the Roman Pontiff can, and ought to, reconcile himself, and come to terms with progress, liberalism and modern civilization" (no. 80). Now, 101 years later (December 7, 1965), the Vatican Council boldly declared in *Gaudium et spes* that the "joy and hope, the grief and anguish of the men of our time" was identical with "the joy and hope, the grief and anguish of the followers of Christ as well" (no. 1). In the second half of the 19th century, as Owen Chadwick has noted, "Many western Europeans had the sensation, not just that the Pope was wrong, but he was morally wrong."[92] A century later, the Church seemed to regain its moral footing. It wanted, like Christ, "to save and not to judge, to serve and not to be served" (no. 3).

What can account for such a remarkable reversal? Out of many factors, I want here to single out only one: the theological reflections of those who had genuinely suffered "the grief and anguish" of the 20th century. Pierre Teilhard de Chardin, Henri de Lubac, and Karl Rahner serve nicely as examples of a much larger cohort (including, among others, Yves Congar and Edward Schillebeeckx). Teilhard de Chardin's embrace of temporality was adopted by the council. Echoing Henri de Lubac, the Church acknowledged legitimate questions and criticisms posed by Communism and atheism. Like Karl Rahner, the council adopted the language of philosophical existentialism, the most potent language of postwar humanism. These modern *mentalités* pressed the council to "return to the sources"—in this case, to restate fundamental questions of historical humanity in terms of "big questions" employing the epideictic genre.

Ecclesiastical authorities had consistently denied Teilhard de Chardin permission to publish his work, but Nicholas Boyle has observed that Teilhard's thought, although "not always appreciated at the time," is the "subterranean influence" on *Gaudium et spes*.[93] As early as 1925, Teilhard had been investigated by the Holy Office, asked to sign six propositions—"I weighed up the enormous scandal and damage that an act of indiscipline on my part would have caused"—and had his licence to teach at the Institut Catholique permanently revoked.[94] Ecclesiastical permission was denied in 1944 to publish *The Phenomenon of Man*. In 1948 it was denied yet again (along with *The Human Zoological Group*). In addition, Teilhard was forbidden to accept the chair in prehistory at the Collège de France, recently vacated by Abbé Breuil.[95] In 1951, fearing that his works would never be published after his death, Teilhard—"backed by legal advice from the resident Jesuit canon lawyer"—designated Mademoiselle Jeanne Mortier his literary executrix and willed all rights over his nonscientific writings to her. A year before Teilhard's death, the Jesuit general put it bluntly: "There is no need to spread these ideas any further."[96]

After Teilhard's death (in American exile) freed his work from ecclesiastical control, the Paris publishing house Seuil immediately began printing his collected works.[97] Dates of publication demonstrate how the first nine volumes, although written years and in some cases even decades earlier, appeared all at once, making for maximal effect on preconciliar consciousness: *Le phénomène humain* (1955); *L'apparition de l'homme* (1956); *La vision du passé* (1957); *Le milieu divin* (1957); *L'avenir de l'homme* (1959); *L'énergie humaine* (1962); *L'activation de l'énergie* (1963); *La place de l'homme dans la nature* (1963); *Science et Christ* (1965).

In 1958, Seuil had published a small volume with the title *Construire la Terre = Building the Earth*.[98] Bearing the notation "extracts from unpublished works," this slim volume was multilingual, containing the French text along with translations into English, German, Russian, and Arabic. It launched Teilhard's work into the world beyond France. English and German editions of his collected works began appearing in 1958; Polish translations followed.[99] A sure sign of Teilhard's increasing influence can be seen in his being censured (posthumously) by the Holy Office on June 30, 1962. This was followed the next day by an anonymous negative critique in *L'Osservatore Romano* of Henri de Lubac's *La pensée religieuse du père Pierre Teilhard de Chardin* (1962). This was the state of affairs just four months prior to the opening of Vatican II.[100]

Why did this flood of publications contribute to a sea change in Catholic thought? If we concentrate on what had been at the heart of Teilhard's theological difficulties—i.e., explaining the doctrine of original sin—we can lose sight of the overwhelmingly larger issue. As early as 1922, Teilhard had experienced difficulty in reconciling his scientific findings with traditional doctrine.[101] Although Pope Pius XII's encyclical *Humani generis* (1950) had opened the door to accepting the possibility of evolution, it had explicitly noted and condemned any acceptance of polygenism as well as any alterations to the doctrine of original sin—"which proceeds from a sin actually committed by an individual Adam and which through generation is passed on to all and is in everyone as his own."[102]

However, this particular doctrinal question, important as it might be, obscured the deeper impact of Teilhard's thought, namely, an embrace of temporality—the fact of *change* in human history—and, as a corollary, of the importance of terrestrial existence in salvation history. The shift from a cyclical or static view of human existence to a notion of an always accelerating linear history had taken place gradually between 1500 and 1800. Reinhart Koselleck identifies this shift as the "temporalization (*Verzeitlichung*) of history" that characterizes "modernity" (*Neuzeit*).[103]

Perhaps the most salient example of this evolving temporalization was the 18th-century inversion of the meaning of "revolution." The term had once indicated a "circulation" around a fixed center and a return to a point of departure: "All variation, or change, *rerum commutatio, rerum conversio,* was insufficient to introduce anything novel into the political world."[104] After 1789 this meaning of "revolution" became barely comprehensible. A "revolution" now signaled a "revolt"—leaving behind a past for a future that was teleologically more advanced—intellectually and morally—than what had been "before." Reactionary Catholic thought, by contrast, clung tenaciously to a classicist model of time and human history in the wake of the French Revolution. As the royalist critic Julien Louis Geoffroy wrote in 1800: "Not only does human reason not perfect itself with time, but this perfection is impossible. It would be necessary to discover new relationships among men, new duties, new moral truths—something that cannot take place in the wake of the Gospel. . . . Nothing beyond Christian morality has been discovered. It is evident that it is the *non plus ultra* of true philosophy, that it is beyond the capacity of human faculties to go farther."[105] If anything, concluded Geoffroy, history taught that the notion of human perfectibility was a "fatal chimera" that had "covered the earth in blood and crimes." Social cohesion depended on clinging to inherited customs, traditions, and beliefs.[106]

This fear of modernity, exemplified most fully in the fear of historicism, shaped ultramontanist Catholicism—a "supernaturalist eternalism"—that was the official face of the Church from at least 1831 until 1958.[107] There had been a golden age and then there was a fall. Human history was a cyclical effort to realize those lost ideals—not entirely futile but also never perfect. Catholicism was not alone in using a postrevolutionary language of decline. Fellow-travelers included Arthur de Gobineau, Jacob Burckhardt, Friedrich Nietzsche, Henry and Brooks Adams, Oswald Spengler, Arnold Toynbee, and German-Jewish intellectuals who likewise feared historicism's erosion of the sacred.[108]

It was only in 1966, one year after the council's conclusion, that Bernard Lonergan explicitly considered the Church's transition from a classicist worldview to historical-mindedness—one in which "intentionality, meaning, is a constitutive component of human living" and "not fixed, static, immutable, but shifting, developing, going astray, capable of redemption." Lonergan's verdict about the "Gospel" repudiated Geoffroy's (in 1800, above) with no less apodictic force: "I think our Scripture scholars would agree that (classicism's) abstractness, and the omissions due to abstraction, have no foundation in the revealed word of God."[109]

Teilhard was uniquely positioned to attempt a reconciliation of these views: he was a scientist, a believer, and perhaps most importantly, a survivor of World War I's trenches. As a scientist he had to reconcile belief in divine providence with the brutal competition and tragic waste inherent in the evolutionary process of natural selection. As a soldier serving as a stretcher-bearer—France quite cynically called back its exiled members of male religious orders to serve the *patrie*'s "sacred union"[110]—Teilhard had seen the very worst that human beings can do to one another. Two of his younger brothers were killed in the war, and Teilhard found himself writing his grief-stricken parents "the usual pained and helpless platitudes."[111]

Yet, his "faith in life" was at once both unswerving and unflinching. Writing from the wartime front on the eve of one more Great War massacre, Teilhard summarized his fundamental faith: "When every certainty is shaken and every utterance falters, when every principle appears doubtful, then there is only one ultimate belief on which we can base our rudderless interior life: the belief *that there is an absolute direction of growth,* to which both our duty and our happiness demand that we should conform; and that *life advances in that direction,* taking the most direct road . . . *life is never mistaken,* either about its road or its destination." At the same time, however, he affirmed that the life-principle was one of struggle, not acquiescence. He recalled having been tempted once by an inner voice whispering, "Take the easier road." But suddenly it "was then that faith in life saved" him. He had realized that "it is not by drifting down the current of things that we shall be united with their one, single, soul, but by fighting our way, with them, toward some goal still to come."[112]

It was this affirmation of terrestrial history that came to him during the war, at once tragic and yet unshakeable, that a generation four decades later eagerly sought in Teilhard's posthumous publications. Freed by death from the reach of ecclesiastical censors, these writings seemed fresh in a world that had survived yet another world war and now lived beneath the mushroom cloud of the Cold War.

Like his friend Teilhard who had comforted those shaken by science, Henri de Lubac also extended his reach beyond the confines of the Church. De Lubac had also returned from exile to serve France in World War I, and he suffered an injury that would cause pain throughout his life. Pierre Rousselot, a fellow Jesuit who had an enormous intellectual influence on de Lubac, was killed in the war.[113] Following the war, de Lubac began in 1924 to work on what would become *Surnaturel* (1946).[114] In 1932, he stated his position succinctly: "Moreover, this concept of a pure nature runs into great difficulties, the principal one of which seems to me to be the following: how can a conscious spirit be anything other than an absolute desire for God?"[115] In 1934, he wrote his "Remarks on the History of the Word, 'Supernatural.'" In 1936, his essay on "Some Aspects of Buddhism" made a remarkable claim: "with the exception of the unique Fact in which we adore the vestige and the very Presence of God, Buddhism is without doubt the greatest spiritual fact in the history of man."[116]

During the German occupation of France in the Vichy years, de Lubac worked with other Jesuits of the Fourvière theologate at Lyons in service of France's "spiritual Resistance." In 1940 he fled the approaching German army. From 1941 to 1944, he was one of the principal theologians collaborating in the clandestine *Cahiers du témoignage chrétien* (Notebooks of Christian Witness).[117] In 1943, hunted by the Gestapo, he successfully escaped to Vals, but his fellow Jesuit Yves de Montcheuil was captured, incarcerated, and executed.[118] ("I have let myself digress at length," de Lubac wrote later. "I have seldom thought of those terrible years.")[119] John Milbank summarizes the theo-political situation: "And it is vital to grasp that de Lubac's and de Montcheuil's *political* opponents— Catholic Rightists supporting the Vichy regime and collaborating with the occupying Germans—were also their *theological* opponents, who reported what they regarded as dubious theological opinions as well as their dubious secular involvements back up the chains of Jesuit and Dominican command to Rome itself."[120]

During the Occupation, de Lubac published parts of what would become *The Drama of Atheist Humanism*. In his preface, poignantly signed "Christmas 1943," he affirmed (like Teilhard) both a thoroughly realistic yet unswerving faith in temporality and terrestrial life: "faith disturbs us and continually upsets the too beautiful balance of our mental conceptions and our social structures. Bursting into a world that perpetually tends to close in upon itself, God brings it the possibility of a harmony that is certainly superior but is to be attained only at the cost of a series of cleavages and struggles coextensive with time itself. . . . The earth, which without God could cease being a chaos only to become a prison, is in reality the magnificent and painful field where our eternal being is worked out."[121]

Atheist humanism for de Lubac was "not to be confused with a hedonist and coarsely materialist atheism," nor with "an atheism of despair" to which it was "quite contrary in principle." The problem posed by it was "a human problem—it was *the* human problem— and the solution that is being given to it is one that claims to be positive."[122] Although de Lubac's work was primarily aimed at critiquing atheism, it found a great deal to admire in the search for a genuine postrationalist humanism. Friedrich Nietzsche was an unlikely ally in his critique of historicism, a derivative form of rationalism, and de Lubac shared Nietzsche's convictions expressed in the *Birth of Tragedy*: "But man starved of myths is a man without roots. He is a man who is 'perpetually hungry', an 'abstract' man, devitalized by the ebbing of the sap in him."[123] The keyword for de Lubac was "mystery," and it shared common ground with a Dionysian lack of clarity: "Myth and mystery may both be said to engender a *mystique*, and each provides a way of escape from 'the prison of things that are clear.'" In the end, while de Lubac sided with mystery (Gabriel Marcel) and *mystique* (Charles Péguy) against "myth," he nevertheless maintained his alliance with Nietzsche against the rationalism of "Socrates, or modern man."[124] In his small volume *Affrontements mystiques* (1950) published after the war, de Lubac included a chapter eventually found in the fourth edition of *Atheist Humanism*: "Nietzsche as Mystic." Here he was able to join old interests with current ones as he expounded on Nietzsche's "European Buddhism." "Without a doubt," wrote de Lubac approvingly, "he exalts life instead of sterilizing it. He seeks the central point from which all of life springs forth, not the central point where all of life is extinguished."[125]

"It was in June 1950 that lightning struck Fourvière," de Lubac would later write.[126] As the Holy Office began its crackdown on theologians associated with *nouvelle théologie*,[127] the Jesuit general ordered de Lubac to stop teaching, to stop working at *Recherches de science religieuse*, and to withdraw three of his books and several essays—including *Surnaturel* (1946) and *De la connaissance de Dieu* (1945; 1948)—from Jesuit libraries and further publication.[128] (There is disagreement over the relationship between this censorship and the promulgation of *Humani generis* [1950].)[129] It seems that two main aspects of de Lubac's thought were unacceptable at the time. First, he insisted that for the human being, there is no independent "natural" world; there is only the one world in which humanity's "supernatural" existence is worked out. (In *Atheist Humanism*, his remarks linking Nietzsche and Kierkegaard were titled "Deeper Immersion in Existence.")[130] Second, and somewhat paradoxically, he emphasized divine immanence precisely to preserve transcendence—that is, to prevent the "mystery" of both humanity and God from being reduced to rationally explicable clarity.

Both aspects of de Lubac's thought—"mystery" and "supernatural"—would later find a place in documents of the council. Meanwhile, throughout the 1950s, his description of Kierkegaard could very well have been applied to him. "It is sufficient that this freelance, outlawed by his Church, was the witness chosen by God to compel a world that increasingly disowned it to contemplate the greatness of faith; that, in a century carried away by immanentism, he was the herald of transcendence."[131]

If de Lubac's Christian humanism had existentialist overtones, Karl Rahner's was more explicitly so. His "Christian pessimism,"[132] intellectually grounded in his 1930s exposure to existentialism—his study with Martin Heidegger was a lasting influence on his thought—would be filled out with experience as a German in World War II. (Heidegger, Rahner later wrote, "developed an important philosophy of Being. That can and will always have a fascinating significance for a Catholic theologian, for whom God is and remains the inexpressible Mystery.")[133] In 1939 the Nazis dissolved the Jesuit College in Innsbruck; Jesuits were placed under a "district prohibition." Rahner accepted a position at the Pastoral Institute in Vienna, a group whose theological work and pastoral care worked against the Nazis. As the Allied front advanced, Rahner moved from Vienna to Lower Bavaria, spending July 1944 to August 1945 caring for villagers and refugees in Mariakirchen.[134] On February 2, 1945, Alfred Delp, Rahner's younger fellow Jesuit to whom he had taught Latin, would be executed by the German Reich. (Delp's work on the philosophy of Heidegger, *Tragische Existenz* [Tragic Existence], was published in 1935. Although Rahner later criticized it for misunderstanding Heidegger, he nonetheless considered Delp to have been in "the front ranks of those witnesses who were motivated by Christianity to resist the evils of Nazism.")[135]

Rahner survived and immersed himself in the task of reconciling Christian faith with a modern consciousness radically altered by the war. Throughout the 1950s he would be subject to occasional censures for his thought; in March 1961, an intervention by Pope John XXIII averted a more serious censure of Rahner by the Vatican.

However, on June 7, 1962, quite unexpectedly—and just three weeks before the Holy Office's posthumous censure of Teilhard (June 30, 1962) and *L'Osservatore Romano*'s assault on de Lubac—Rahner's Jesuit superiors "informed him that from now on everything that he wrote had to be submitted to a preliminary censorship in Rome."[136] Rahner told the Jesuit general that he "had no intention of submitting anything to the Roman censorship but would rather write nothing at all; nor would [he] keep quiet about the matter, but would describe it all quite candidly."[137] By May 28, 1963, the Holy Office had retreated completely. In the meantime, Rahner had been nominated by John XXIII as a council *peritus*, and he became the private adviser on all council documents for Cardinals König and Döpfner. By 1964, Rahner had come to be regarded by a number of friends and foes as "the most powerful man" at the council.[138]

While the "existentialist" or Heideggerian aspect of Rahner's thought might be systematized more thoroughly in his large academic works (especially *Hearers of the Word* [1969] and *Foundations of Christian Faith* [1978]), it comes across with greatest immediacy in sermons delivered in the rubble of the war's aftermath. In Lent 1946, while teaching at the Jesuit philosophy faculty in Munich, Rahner preached sermons at St. Michael's Church.[139] He appealed to the vivid memories of Allied firebombing (recently the subject of great controversy[140]) and his parishioners' traumatic experience of terror.

Do you remember the nights in the cellar, the nights of deadly loneliness amidst the harrowing crush of people? The nights of helplessness and of waiting for a senseless death? The nights when the lights went out, when horror and impotence gripped one's heart, when one mimed being courageous and unaffected? . . . When one finally gave up, when one became silent, when one only waited hopelessly for the end, death? Alone, powerless, empty. And if the cellar really became buried by rubble, then the picture of today's man is complete.[141]

Rahner's concrete description of existential isolation—of *Dasein*'s being "thrown" into a historical existence without whence or whither—seemed to invite the most despairing kind of pessimism. But this was a rhetorical prelude to a description of humanity's common destiny as the necessary starting point for religious experience:

> For such are we people of today, even if we already have crawled out of the rubbled-over cellars, even if our everyday has already begun again. . . . We men of today are still the rubbled-over because as such we have already entered into an exterior destiny, because the exterior destiny . . . is only the shadow of events which have occurred in the depths of men: that their hearts are rubbled-over.[142]

And what must one do after finding oneself in such a situation of the "rubbled-over heart"? One must "stand firm and submit to it." This is the beginning of true faith, of being "freed into the freedom of the infinite God." Admittedly, being rubbled-over can also lead to an atheistic humanism, but the twilight of the gods can also lead further to the one true God. Those in despair "curse, they hate themselves and the world and say there is no God. They say there is no God because they confuse the true God with what they held to be their God. And they are actually right in their opinion. The God that they meant really does not exist." These people do not understand their own despair correctly, for "they saw in it the death of God and not his true advent."[143]

Thus Rahner counsels: "In this occurrence of the heart, let despair take everything away from you, in truth you will only lose the finite and the futile, no matter how great and wonderful it was, even if it is you yourself . . . you with your image of God which resembled you instead of the Incomprehensible himself. Whatever can be taken from you is never God." Perhaps slyly alluding to Sartre's *No Exit* (1944), Rahner adds: "Let all your exits be blocked, only the exits to the finite will be rubbled-over and the ways into the really futile." When all of this is accepted, one will find oneself "laid in the hands of this God, this Father whose deadly decree became love."[144]

In the sermons that follow, Rahner uses pastoral language to visit themes like those considered by de Lubac. In the "recent decades of European intellectual history," thinkers considered the human being "to be free, unbound, limitless, only responsible to the inner law of his nature, to be the autonomous person." But what is this "I" that "notices nothing and is devoid of this Spirit? This I does not exist at all, the I that doesn't have *more* in it than what even the outermost surface of our nature, that we usually call our consciousness, can oversee. This I is an abstraction of the Enlightenment's philistine of the nineteenth century. Who am 'I' then? I am in truth the man of infinite possibilities, enormous abysses, incalculable expanses!" If both the human being and God are mystery, then we must immerse ourselves in existence: "God must be sought and found *in* the world, therefore the everyday must become God's day, going out into the world must become going inward with God, the everyday must become a 'day of recollection.' The everyday itself must be prayed."[145]

Rahner would also, like de Lubac, concern himself with what Archbishop Denis Hurley of South Africa called "the central theological problem of the century," namely, the relationship of the natural order to humanity's supernatural end. The creature, Rahner wrote, "is endowed, by virtue of its inmost essence and constitution, with the possibility of being assumed, of being the material of a possible history of God."[146] Conciliar passages that reflect his existentialist outlook offer little solace to readers looking for sentimental certitude: "It was completely alien to Rahner to lull hopeful, seeking or perplexed people to prayer with comforting words, or to envelop real problems of life in a religious mist."[147] But to those who had experienced the very worst that the bloodiest of centuries had to offer, Rahner's honest acknowledgment of humanity's "rubbled-over" condition had a solace all its own—the consolation that comes from being understood and not dismissed. As for the Germans after the war—those who lived in a divided country that was ground zero for a nuclear confrontation—existential angst was not neurosis. It was simply an appropriate response to life in the Atomic Age.

Content: Taking Temporality Seriously
or, What Is Salvation?

The themes of temporality, existentialism, and atheism emerge most movingly in *Gaudium et spes*. Not coincidentally, this document—although it was criticized by some for not having a developed notion of sin—differs markedly from the earlier decrees by explicitly admitting anxiety over human fragmentation. In its introduction, addressing "The Situation of Man in the World Today," the council spoke about *both* hope *and* "anguish" within the context of an unprecedented temporal epoch. It began with a classically Marxist analysis of the base-superstructure relationship: "Ours is a new age of history with critical and swift upheavals spreading gradually to all corners of the earth. They are the products of man's intelligence and creative activity, but they recoil upon him, upon his judgments and desires, both individual and collective, upon his ways of thinking and acting in regard to people and things." It continued with Marx's notion of the producer's "alienation" from the product: "Increase in power is not always accompanied by control of that power for the benefit of man." It concluded with the anxiety that comes from a human person's being thrown into "the laws of social living": "man often seems more uncertain than ever of himself . . . he is perplexed by uncertainty" (no. 4).

The passage continues with the paradoxes of the present: "*In no other age* has mankind enjoyed such an abundance . . . and yet a huge proportion of the people of the world is plagued. . . . *At no time* have men had such a keen sense of freedom, only to be faced by new forms of slavery. . . . There is on the one hand *a lively feeling of unity and of compelling solidarity*, of mutual dependence, and on the other *a lamentable cleavage of bitterly opposing camps*. We have not yet seen the last of bitter political, social, and economic hostility, and racial and ideological antagonism, nor are we free from the spectre of *a war of total destruction*." As a result, contemporaries "hover between *hope* and *anxiety* and *wonder uneasily* about the present course of events. It is a situation that challenges men to respond; *they cannot escape*" (no. 4). This analysis succinctly presents a theology of *crisis*—of Heideggerian dread, Sartrean authenticity, and a Kierkegaardian demand for decision.

The influence of Teilhard de Chardin is felt keenly at this point under the rubric "deep-seated changes," and it marks a turning point in Catholic thought from classicism to historical-mindedness. First comes a seeming allusion to Teilhard's notion of a noosphere, a global unifying of intelligence that brings with it a corollary demand for taking responsibility: "The human mind is, in a certain sense, broadening mastery over time." Then follows a sense of what Alvin Toffler's best-seller would soon call *Future Shock* (1970):[148] "The accelerated pace of history is such that one can scarcely keep abreast of it." Finally comes an acknowledgment of the need to accept modernity's sense of temporalization: "And so mankind substitutes a dynamic and more evolutionary concept of nature for a static one." Realizing that such a radical change in worldview comes with costs, the passage immediately reinforces the notions of anxiety and decision: "the result is an immense series of new problems calling for a new endeavor of analysis and synthesis" (no. 5). The double bind of modernization and modernity is summed up in a thoroughly Teilhardian declaration: "Man is growing conscious that the forces he has unleashed are in his own hands and that it is up to him to control them or be enslaved by them. Here lies the modern dilemma" (no. 9).

Poignantly, the document immediately moves from this structuralist approach to an existentialist one. Under the heading, "Man's deeper questionings," the focus shifts to the interior: "The dichotomy affecting the modern world is, in fact, a symptom of the deeper dichotomy that is in man himself. He is the meeting point of many conflicting forces." Once again comes the Kierkegaardian analysis of dread: "In his condition as a created being he is subject to a thousand shortcomings, but feels untrammeled in his inclination and destined for a higher form of life." This human dualism— the condition of being both an angel and a beast—leads to dread and decision: "Torn by a welter of anxieties he is compelled to choose between them and repudiate some among them." However, as St. Paul says, a person "often does the very thing he hates and does not do what he wants. And so he feels himself divided." Being thus reminded of humanity's irreducible bind, the council invokes the big questions: "there is a growing body of men who are asking the most fundamental of all questions or are glimpsing them with a keener insight: What is man? What is the meaning of suffering, evil, death, which have not been eliminated by all this progress? . . . What happens after this earthly life is ended?" The section ends with a nod to de Lubac: "that is why the Council . . . proposes to speak to all men in order *to unfold the mystery that is man*" (no. 10).

The following chapter, "The Dignity of the Human Person," sets out the question: "But what is man?" Depending on whether one emphasizes the angel or the beast, "he either sets himself up as the absolute measure of all things, or debases himself to the point of despair. Hence his *doubt* and his *anguish*" (no. 12). There is a dignity to human intellect, truth, conscience, and freedom. But there is also "The Mystery of Death," and it is in this regard "that man's condition is most shrouded in *doubt*. Man is tormented not only by pain and by the gradual breaking-up of his body but also, and even more, by the *dread* of forever ceasing to be" (no. 18).

Having taken pains to acknowledge just how much modern consciousness is marked by what Ernest Becker would soon call *The Denial of Death* (1973),[149] the document turns to "Kinds of Atheism and Its Causes" and declares: "Atheism must therefore be regarded as one of the most serious problems of our time, and one that deserves more thorough treatment." In its delineation of the strands of atheism the document echoed Rahner's 1946 sermons preached in the rubble: "Yet others have such a false notion of God that when they disown this product of the imagination their denial has no reference to the God of the Gospels." Remarkably, the council here reversed over a century of combative rhetoric[150] by placing some of the responsibility for the modern situation on the shoulders of Christians: "But believers themselves often share some responsibility for this situation. . . . To the extent that they are careless about their instruction in the faith, or present its teaching falsely, or even fail in their religious, moral, or social life, they must be said to conceal rather than to reveal the true nature of God and of religion" (no. 19).

More importantly, it took the criticisms of atheism seriously: "Well knowing how important are the problems raised by atheism . . .

she considers that these motives deserve an honest and more thorough scrutiny." Instead of simplistic condemnations, it returned to deep sources where belief and unbelief originate: "Meanwhile, every man remains a question to himself, one that is dimly perceived and left unanswered. For there are times, especially in the major events of life, when no man can altogether escape from such self-questioning." Where belief and unbelief eventually part company is in the decision to embrace or reject mystery: "God alone, who calls man to deeper thought and to more humble probing, can fully and with complete certainty supply an answer to this questioning." Realizing that atheism is a fact of modernity, the council urges both parties to transcend their differences over belief and step back to see pressing terrestrial needs: "Although the Church altogether rejects atheism, she nevertheless sincerely proclaims that all men, those who believe as well as those who do not, should help establish right order in this world where all live together" (no. 21).

In its prelude to consideration of practical problems needing urgent attention, the chapter entitled "Man's Activity in the Universe" begins once again with the posing of big questions: "In the face of this immense enterprise now involving the whole human race men are troubled by many questionings. What is the meaning and value of this feverish activity? How ought all of these things be used? To what goal is all this individual and collective enterprise heading?" (no. 33). It is in the light of these questions that the council defined its "salvific purpose" in modern times: first, to "communicate divine life to men"; second, to cast "the reflected light of that divine life over all the earth"—that is, as a light to the nations. The Church "believes it can contribute much to *humanizing* the family of man and its history," above all in three ways: (1) "in the way it heals and elevates the *dignity of the human person*"; (2) "in the way it *consolidates society*"; and, in a direct response to the large questions raised above, (3) in the way that it "endows the daily activity of men with a *deeper sense and meaning*" (no. 40). As Rahner had preached in the rubble of 1946: "if we let ourselves be taken by the everyday . . . then the everyday is no longer the everyday, then it is prayer."[151]

What is salvation? And what is the "salvific purpose" of the Church? By the time the council had come to its conclusion in

December 1965, it had arrived at a remarkably different place than where it had begun in 1962. While not neglecting the details of the Church's internal life, it had stepped back from perspectives specific to Catholicism, Christianity, and even religion in general. It had stepped back to see the world—humanity, history, existence—from the perspective of the broadest possible horizons. It asked anew what its purpose was—and what the purpose of Christian believers was—in a world populated by nations and cultures whose difference and diversity were finally being acknowledged in a postcolonialist world. Speaking in the modern dialects of science, existentialism, atheism, and historical-mindedness, it situated itself as a dialogue partner with a bloc of nonbelievers (in both West and East) whose questions could no longer simply be condemned or dismissed.

Conclusion

This new language—a language of going "back to the sources" not only of faith but of human existence itself—was not merely novel. It was an ethical necessity. It was a consequence of gathering representatives from all over the decolonized globe in the years 1962 to 1965, a time in which no one could have known whether "the world's deepest anxieties"—that is, the annihilation of the human race—were going to be realized or not.

Now that the Cold War is being forgotten by those who lived through it and is practically unknown to those who did not, it is too easy—and, for some, suspiciously expedient—to forget what it had once been like to be compelled by anxiety to return to sources. But it should not be forgotten, not by unwitting ignorance or willful amnesia. We should remember it not only for the sake of truth. We should remember it for the sake of the good.

The council's call for the Church to be a "humanizing" force was an ethically necessary response to a century that had been, in Nietzsche's ironic phrase, "human, all too human." The form was appropriate to the context: a magnanimous voice, rising above all pusillanimity, calling people back to the fundamental questions and evoking generosity and goodwill. Of all the reasons it did this, none stands out so boldly as the anxiety of those "Thirteen Days" in

October 1962 that eerily coincided with—and set the defining stage for—the council's first hours:

> Warned by the possibility of the catastrophes that man has created, let us profit by the respite we now enjoy, thanks to the divine favor, to take stock of our responsibilities and find ways of resolving controversies in a manner worthy of human beings. Providence urgently demands of us that we free ourselves from the age-old slavery of war. If we refuse to make this effort, there is no knowing where we will be led on the fatal path we have taken (*Gaudium et spes* no. 81).

Notes

I want to thank David Collins, S.J., Michael C. McCarthy, S.J., Mark O'Connor, John W. O'Malley, S.J., Virginia Reinburg, and Todd Romero for valuable references and suggestions. I am grateful to the LoSchiavo Chair in Catholic Social Thought at the University of San Francisco for making this study possible.

* All quotations from the documents of Vatican II are cited in the text by paragraph number and taken from *Vatican II: The Conciliar and Post Conciliar Documents. Study Edition*, ed. Austin Flannery, O.P. (Northport, N.Y.: Costello, 1987). All emphases added.

1. Paul Ricoeur, *Memory, History, Forgetting*, trans. Kathleen Blamey and David Pellauer (Chicago: Chicago University, 2004) 506.

2. François Furet, *The Passing of an Illusion: The Idea of Communism in the Twentieth Century*, trans. Deborah Furet (Chicago: University of Chicago, 1999).

3. "Every Monday and Wednesday afternoon each fall semester I lecture to several hundred Yale undergraduates on the subject of Cold War history. As I do this, I have to keep reminding myself that hardly any of them remember any of the events I'm describing. When I talk about Stalin and Truman, even Reagan

and Gorbachev, it could as easily be Napoleon, Caesar, or Alexander the Great. Most members of the Class of 2005, for example, were only five years old when the Berlin Wall came down. . . . For this first post-Cold War generation, then, the Cold War is at once distant and dangerous. What could anyone ever have had to fear, they wonder, from a state that turned out to be as weak, as bumbling, and as *temporary* as the Soviet Union? But they also ask themselves and me: how did we ever make it out of the Cold War alive?" John Lewis Gaddis, *The Cold War: A New History* (New York: Penguin, 2005) ix–x.

4. Gaddis, *The Cold War* 266.

5. On memory, monuments, and memorialization, see Stephen Schloesser, *Jazz Age Catholicism: Mystic Modernism in Postwar Paris, 1919–1933* (Toronto: University of Toronto, 2005) 10, 330–331 nn. 31–35.

6. Ernest Renan, "What Is a Nation?" (1882), in *Nation and Narration*, ed. Homi Bhabha (New York: Routledge, 1990) 11.

7. John W. O'Malley, "Vatican II: Did Anything Happen?" above at 76.

8. Ibid. 74.

9. Ibid. 55.

10. Ibid. 56.

11. For other attempts to sketch the historical background of the council see Étienne Fouilloux, "The Antepreparatory Phase: The Slow Emergence from Inertia (January, 1959–October, 1962)," in *History of Vatican II*, ed. Giuseppe Alberigo and Joseph A. Komonchak, vol. 1, *Announcing and Preparing Vatican Council II: Toward a New Era in Catholicism* (Maryknoll, N.Y.: Orbis, 1995) 55–166, esp. 55–60; and Giacomo Martina, "The Historical Context in Which the Idea of a New Ecumenical Council Was Born," in *Vatican II: Assessment and Perspectives Twenty-Five Years After (1962–1987)*, ed. René Latourelle, 3 vols. (New York: Paulist, 1988) 1:3–73.

12. For this method of paying attention to textual repetition and repression, see, for example: Michel Foucault, *The History of Sexuality, vol. 1, An Introduction*, trans. Robert Hurley (New York: Pantheon, 1978) esp. 32–35; Joan Scott, *Gender and the*

Politics of History (New York: Columbia University, 1988) esp. 7–9; Gavin I. Langmuir, *History, Religion, and Antisemitism* (Berkeley: University of California, 1990) esp. 252–71.

13. Stephen Kern, *The Culture of Space and Time, 1880–1918* (Cambridge, Mass.: Harvard University, 1983); David Harvey, *The Condition of Postmodernity: An Enquiry into the Origins of Cultural Change* (New York: Blackwell, 1989).

14. Kern, *Culture of Space and Time* 66.

15. Pierre Granet, *L'Evolution des méthodes diplomatiques* (Paris: A. Rousseau, 1939); in Kern, *Culture of Space and Time* 275.

16. Modris Eksteins, *Rites of Spring: The Great War and the Birth of the Modern Age* (Boston: Houghton Mifflin, 1989) 98.

17. Eyewitness account by Harry Crosby, American veteran of Verdun, in Eksteins, *Rites of Spring* 243; for Lindbergh, see 242–52, 261–67.

18. Gaddis, *Cold War* 68.

19. Ibid. 95.

20. Ibid. 83; quoting Bohlen memorandum dated August 30, 1947.

21. Ibid. 65.

22. Ibid. 70.

23. Xavier Rynne, *Vatican Council II* (Maryknoll, N.Y.: Orbis, (1999; orig. publ. 1968) 56–66.

24. Henri Fesquet, *The Drama of Vatican II: The Ecumenical Council, June 1962–December 1965,* trans. Bernard Murchland (New York: Random House, 1967) 40.

25. Gerald P. Fogarty, "The Council Gets Underway," in *History of Vatican II,* vol. 2, *The Formation of the Council's Identity: First Period and Intersession, October 1962–September 1963,* ed. Giuseppe Alberigo and Joseph A. Komonchak (Maryknoll, N.Y.: Orbis, 1997) 69–106, at 94–104.

26. Fogarty, "The Council Gets Underway" 98.

27. John XXIII, *Pacem in terris* (April 11, 1963), in *The Papal Encyclicals,* 5 vols., ed. Claudia Carlen (Raleigh, N.C.: Pierian, 1990) 5:107–129, at 107.

28. Fogarty, "The Council Gets Underway" 104.

29. James Chapman, "The BBC and the Censorship of *The War Game* (1965)," *Journal of Contemporary History* 41 (2006) 75–94.
30. Gaddis, *Cold War* 119–155.
31. "Today we are seeing this revolution of the non-white peoples. . . . What it is, simply, is that black and brown and red and yellow peoples have, after hundreds of years of exploitation and imposed 'inferiority' and general misuse, become, finally, do-or-die sick and tired of the white man's heel on their necks" (Malcolm X, *The Autobiography of Malcolm X as Told to Alex Haley* [New York: Ballantine, 1999; orig. publ. 1965] 299).
32. Gaddis, *Cold War* 120.
33. Edward W. Said, *Orientalism* (New York: Pantheon, 1978) 2.
34. Gail Bederman, *Manliness and Civilization: A Cultural History of Gender and Race in the United States, 1880–1917* (Chicago: University of Chicago, 1995) 23–31; Schloesser, *Jazz Age Catholicism* 25–26; 37–38.
35. Jean Comaroff and John L. Comaroff, *Of Revelation and Revolution*, vol. 1, *Christianity, Colonialism, and Consciousness in South Africa*; vol. 2, *The Dialectics of Modernity on a South African Frontier* (Chicago: University of Chicago, 1991, 1997).
36. Giuseppe Ruggieri, "Beyond an Ecclesiology of Polemics: The Debate on the Church," in *History of Vatican II* 2:281–357, at 285, 286, 293, 294.
37. Joseph A. Komonchak, "The Initial Debate about the Church," in *Vatican II commence—: Approches francophones*, ed. E. Fouilloux (Leuven: Bibliotheek van de Faculteit der Godgeleerdheid, 1993) 329–52.
38. George Minamiki, S.J., *The Chinese Rites Controversy from Its Beginning to Modern Times* (Chicago: Loyola University, 1985) 189.
39. Giovanni Benelli, "Les rapports entre le Siège de Pierre et les églises locals" in *La Documentation Catholique* 60/1644 (16 December 1973) 1072; in Minamiki, *Chinese Rites Controversy* 221. As Minimaki notes, George Dunne pointed out that

Benelli's address was "the first time any high ranking official in Rome has openly admitted that the Roman decision against the rites was wrong. Dunne adds that Benelli in effect makes two statements: "1) the decision contributed to retarding conversion in Asia for centuries—which is to say it was wrong; and 2) it should not have been made in Rome but should have been left to the Church in China, which is in effect to say to the Jesuits in China, to make the decisions" (ibid. 322 n. 41).

40. For example, see: Voltaire's *Treatise on Toleration* (1763); Zalkind Hourwitz's *Vindication of the Jews* (1789); *Petition of the Jews of Paris, Alsace, and Lorraine to the National Assembly* (January 28, 1790); La Fare, Bishop of Nancy, *Opinion on the Admissibility of Jews to Full Civil and Political Rights* (Spring 1790); *Admission of Jews to Rights of Citizenship* (September 27, 1791); all collected in *The French Revolution and Human Rights: A Brief Documentary History*, ed. and trans. Lynn Hunt (Boston: Bedford Books of St. Martin's, 1996).

41. David I. Kertzer, *The Popes against the Jews: The Vatican's Role in the Rise of Modern Anti-Semitism* (New York: Knopf, 2001) 28–30.

42. Alyssa Goldstein Sepinwall, *The Abbé Grégoire and the French Revolution: The Making of Modern Universalism* (Berkeley: University of California, 2005).

43. Abbé Grégoire, in Lynn Hunt, "Introduction: The Revolutionary Origins of Human Rights," in Hunt, *The French Revolution* 1–32, at 9.

44. Michael Broers, *Europe under Napoleon 1799–1815* (New York: Arnold, 1996) 129–30, 113.

45. Kertzer, *Popes against the Jews* 37.

46. David I. Kertzer, *The Kidnapping of Edgardo Mortara* (New York: Vintage, 1997) 118–42.

47. Kertzer, *Popes against the Jews* 129–30; Kertzer, *Prisoner of the Vatican: The Popes' Secret Plot to Capture Rome from the New Italian State* (Boston: Houghton Mifflin, 2004).

48. Pierre Birnbaum, *The Anti-Semitic Moment: A Tour of France in 1898*, trans. Jane Marie Todd (New York: Hill & Wang, 2003).

49. Schloesser, *Jazz Age Catholicism* 50–56. "'We are integral Roman Catholics, they boasted. 'That is, we set above all and everyone not only the Church's traditional teaching in the order of absolute truths but also the pope's directions in the order of practical contingencies. For the Church and the pope are one'" (ibid. 55, quoting *La Vigie* [December 5, 1912]; in Roger Aubert et al., *The Church in a Secularised Society* [New York: Paulist, 1978] 200).

50. Ruth Harris, *Lourdes: Body and Spirit in the Secular Age* (New York: Viking, 1999) 275–79; Pierre Sorlin, *"La Croix" et les Juifs (1880–1899): Contribution à l'histoire de l'antisémitisme contemporain* (Paris: B. Grasset, 1967).

51. Reported in *Time* 151.4 (January 26, 1998) 20.

52. "We know well that the Jew was the inventor of our anti-Christian laws, that he put them on stage like a puppetmaster, concealed behind a curtain, pulling the string which makes the devil appear before an unsuspecting audience. . . . The subtle alliance of the makers of the anti-Christian laws with the powerful Dreyfus syndicate leaves no room for doubt. They are all of a piece. Destroy the army, destroy the religious orders, and let the Jew reign! That is the goal" (*La Croix* [January 28, 1898]; in James Carroll, *Constantine's Sword: The Church and the Jews* [New York: Houghton Mifflin, 2001] 459–60).

53. Gordon Wright, *France in Modern Times*, 5th ed. (New York: Norton, 1995) 250; Aubert et al., *Church in a Secularised Society* 79–80.

54. "To have been in the margins is to have been in contact with danger, to have been a source of power" (Mary Douglas, *Purity and Danger: An Analysis of the Concepts of Pollution and Taboo* [New York: Routledge, 1996; orig. publ. 1966] 98).

55. Giovanni Miccoli, "Two Sensitive Issues: Religious Freedom and the Jews," in *History of Vatican II*, ed. Alberigo and

Komonchak, vol. 4, *Church as Communion* 95–193, esp. 135–93.

56. Michael Phayer, *The Catholic Church and the Holocaust, 1930–1965* (Bloomington: Indiana University, 2000) 184–202.

57. Ibid. 199.

58. Schloesser, *Jazz Age Catholicism* 56–61; 206–8, at 207, 208.

59. Jacques Maritain, in Michael R. Marrus, "The Ambassador & The Pope; Pius XII, Jacques Maritain & the Jews," *Commonweal* 131.18 (October 22, 2004) 14–19, at 16.

60. Phayer, *Catholic Church and the Holocaust* 206.

61. Ibid. 86.

62. Ibid. 208–15.

63. Claude Soetens, "The Ecumenical Commitment of the Catholic Church," in *History of Vatican II*, ed. Alberigo and Komonchak, vol. 3, *Mature Council: Second Period and Intersession, September 1963–September 1964* (Maryknoll, N.Y.: Orbis, 2000) 257–345, esp. 339–45. See also Rynne, *Vatican Council II* 303–5; and Fesquet, *Drama of Vatican II* 357–65.

64. Pope Pius XI, "An Act of Dedication of the Human Race," promulgated in conjunction with the encyclical *Quas primas* (December 11, 1925) on the Feast of Christ the King; in *The Raccolta*, ed. Joseph P. Christopher and Charles E. Spence (New York: Benziger Brothers, 1943) 180–82, at 181.

65. Ibid. 181.

66. General Intercessions for Good Friday, in *The Sacramentary*, the Roman Missal revised by decree of the Second Vatican Council and published by authority of Pope Paul VI, English translation prepared by the International Commission on English in the Liturgy, rev. ed. (New York: Catholic, 1985) 146.

67. Augustine of Hippo, Sermon 112.8; in Augustine, *Sermons*, trans. Edmund Hill, O.P., 11 vols. (Brooklyn: New City, 1990–1997) 4:152 (emphasis original).

68. Edward Peter, *Torture*, exp. ed, (Philadelphia : University of Pennsylvania, 1996).

69. R. I. Moore, *The Formation of a Persecuting Society: Power and Deviance in Western Europe, 950–1250* (New York: Basil Blackwell, 1987).
70. Brad S. Gregory, *Salvation at Stake: Christian Martyrdom in Early Modern Europe* (Cambridge, Mass.: Harvard University, 1999).
71. "Concordat between the Holy See and the Republic of France, 15 July 1801," in *Readings in Church History*, ed. Coleman J. Barry, rev. ed., 3 vols. in 1, (Westminster, Md.: Christian Classics, 1985) 943–45, at 943.
72. Darrin M. McMahon, *Enemies of the Enlightenment: The French Counter-Enlightenment and the Making of Modernity* (New York: Oxford University, 2001).
73. Gregory XVI, "Mirari vos" (August 15, 1832) nos. 14–15; in Carlen, *Papal Encyclicals* 1:235–41, at 238 (emphasis original).
74. Pius IX, *Quanta cura* (December 8, 1864) no. 3; in Carlen, *Papal Encyclicals* 1:381–86, at 382, quoting Gregory XVI, *Mirari vos* (emphasis original).
75. Pius IX, Syllabus of Errors (December 8, 1864); in Barry, *Readings in Church History* 992, 996.
76. Leo XIII, *Libertas* (June 20, 1888) no. 21; in Carlen, *Papal Encyclicals* 2:169–81, at 175.
77. Ibid. no. 33; in Carlen, *Papal Encyclicals* 2:178.
78. Wright, *France in Modern Times* 250; Pius IX, Syllabus of Errors no. 55; in Barry, *Readings in Church History* 995.
79. Pius XII, Christmas Allocution of December 24, 1945, in Barry, *Readings in Church History* 1220–25. This document's positive remarks on democracy were preceded by those in Pius XII's "View on the Spiritual Power of the Church and Contemporary Theories of State Power" (October 2, 1945), but this document was marked by more qualifications than the December text: "If, therefore, the people depart from the Christian faith or do not hold it resolutely as the principle of civil life, even democracy is easily altered and deformed, and in the course of time is liable to fall into a one-party 'totalitarianism' or 'authoritarianism'" (Barry, *Readings in Church History* 1225–30, at 1227–28).

80. Pius XII, Christmas Allocution 1224.
81. John T. Noonan, Jr., *A Church That Can and Cannot Change: The Development of Catholic Moral Teaching* (Notre Dame, Ind.: University of Notre Dame, 2005) 145–58.
82. Cardinal Siri, in Rynne, *Vatican Council II* 460.
83. John T. McGreevy, *Catholicism and American Freedom: A History* (New York: Norton, 2003) 207–8.
84. Quoted in Rynne, *Vatican Council II* 460.
85. Letter of Msgr. John Tracy Ellis to Fr. Edward Cardinal (September 13, 1963); in McGreevy, *Catholicism and American Freedom* 237; for Ellis in 1955, see 207.
86. On "Three Moments for *Dignitatis Humanae*," see Hermínio Rico, S.J., *John Paul II and the Legacy of Dignitatis Humanae* (Washington: Georgetown University, 2002) 1–26. On Eastern European bishops at the council, see for example: Evangelista Vilanova, "The Intersession (1963–1964)," in *History of Vatican II* 3:413–14; and Rynne, *Vatican Council II* 300, 463–64.
87. McMahon, *Enemies of the Enlightenment* 133–38.
88. Kertzer, *Kidnapping of Edgardo Mortara* 147.
89. See, for example: Steven W. Hackel, *Children of Coyote, Missionaries of Saint Francis: Indian-Spanish Relations in Colonial California, 1769–1850* (Chapel Hill: University of North Carolina, 2005); David Wallace Adams, *Education for Extinction: American Indians and the Boarding School Experience, 1875–1928* (Lawrence: University of Kansas, 1995).
90. Marvin R. O'Connell, *Critics on Trial: An Introduction to the Catholic Modernist Crisis* (Washington: Catholic University of America, 1994), 201–4; O'Connell, *John Ireland and the American Catholic Church* (St. Paul: Minnesota Historical Society, 1988).
91. Rynne, *Vatican Council II* 464.
92. Owen Chadwick, *The Secularization of the European Mind in the 19th Century* (New York: Cambridge University, 1975) 111–12.

93. Nicholas Boyle, "On Earth, as It Is in Heaven," *Tablet* 259.8596 (July 9, 2005) 12–15, at 12.

94. Ursula King, *Spirit of Fire: The Life and Vision of Teilhard de Chardin* (Maryknoll, N.Y.: Orbis, 1996) 106–8, at 107.

95. King, *Spirit of Fire* 174, 198–99.

96. Ibid. 196–99, 207, 224; Mary Lukas and Ellen Lukas, *Teilhard: The Man, the Priest, the Scientist* (New York: Doubleday, 1977) 296–98.

97. Teilhard's works appeared from Seuil in the series *Oeuvres de Teilhard de Chardin* from 1955 to 1973 and are listed under individual titles.

98. Pierre Teilhard de Chardin, *Construire la terre = Building the Earth* (Paris: Seuil, 1958).

99. For example, *The Phenomenon of Man*, trans. Bernard Wall (New York: Harper, 1959); *Der Mensch im Kosmos*, trans. Othon Marbach (Munich: Beck, 1959); *Człowiek, struktura i kierunki ewolucji grupy zoologicznej ludzkiej* [*Man's Place in Nature: The Human Zoological Group*], trans. Janina i Grzegorz Fedorowscy (Warsaw: Pax, 1962); *Wybór pism* [*Collected Writings*], 2nd ed., ed. W. Sukiennicka, trans. M. Tazbir (Warsaw: Pax, 1966).

100. Henri de Lubac, *La pensée religieuse du père Pierre Teilhard de Chardin* (Paris: Aubier, 1962). See Fouilloux, "The Anterpreparatory Phase" 75; Joseph A. Komonchak, "The Struggle for the Council during the Preparation of Vatican II (1960–1962)," in *History of Vatican II* 1:167–356; see 243 n. 291; Norman Tanner, "The Church in the World (*Ecclesia ad Extra*)" in *History of Vatican II* 4:269–386, at 285–86.

101. King, *Spirit of Fire* 106.

102. Pius XII, *Humani generis* (August 12, 1950) no. 37, in Carlen, *Papal Encyclicals* 4:175–84, at 182.

103. Reinhart Koselleck, *Futures Past: On the Semantics of Historical Time*, trans. Keith Tribe (Cambridge, Mass.: MIT, 1985) 3–20.

104. See ibid. 39–54, at 41.

105. Julien-Louis Geoffroy, review of Madame de Staël's *De la littérature considérée dans ses rapports avec les institutions sociales* (1800), in McMahon, *Enemies of the Enlightenment* 140.
106. Geoffroy, in McMahon, *Enemies of the Enlightenment* 141; see also 138–45.
107. Schloesser, *Jazz Age Catholicism* 27–35.
108. Arthur Herman, *The Idea of Decline in Western History* (New York: Free Press, 1997); David N. Myers, *Resisting History: Historicism and Its Discontents in German-Jewish Thought* (Princeton, N.J.: Princeton University, 2003).
109. Bernard Lonergan, "The Transition from a Classicist World-View to Historical-Mindedness," an address delivered at a meeting of the Canon Law Society of America in 1966; in Bernard J. F. Lonergan, *A Second Collection: Papers*, ed. William F. J. Ryan and Bernard J. Tyrrell (Toronto: University of Toronto, 1996; orig. publ. 1974) 1–9, at 6, 5.
110. Schloesser, *Jazz Age Catholicism* 84, 105.
111. Lukas and Lukas, *Teilhard* 46, 55.
112. Pierre Teilhard de Chardin, "Cosmic Life," in *Writings in Time of War* (New York: Harper & Row, 1968) 28–32; in *Pierre Teilhard de Chardin*, ed. Ursula King (Maryknoll, N.Y.: Orbis, 1999) 48–49 (emphasis original).
113. John Milbank, *The Suspended Middle: Henri de Lubac and the Debate concerning the Supernatural* (Grand Rapids, Mich.: Eerdmans, 2005) 3.
114. See David L. Schindler, "Introduction to the 1998 Edition," in Henri de Lubac, S.J., *The Mystery of the Supernatural*, trans. Rosemary Sheed (New York: Crossroad, (1998; orig. publ. 1966) xvi–xvii n. 18; Michel Sales, "Préface," in Henri de Lubac, *Surnaturel: Études historiques*, ed. Michel Sales (Paris: Desclée de Brouwer, (1991; orig. publ. 1946) i–xvi.
115. Letter of Henri de Lubac to Maurice Blondel (April 3, 1932), in Milbank, *Suspended Middle* viii.
116. Henri de Lubac, *Aspects du bouddhisme* (Paris: Seuil, 1951) 18; in Schindler, "Introduction" xiv.

117. Henri de Lubac, "The Spirit of the *Cahiers du Témoignage chrétien*," in *Christian Resistance to Anti-Semitism: Memories from 1940–1944*, trans. Sister Elizabeth Englund, O.C.D. (San Francisco: Ignatius, 1990) 131–45.

118. *Three Jesuits Speak: Yves de Montcheuil, 1899–1944, Charles Nicolet, 1897–1961, Jean Zupan, 1899–1968: Characteristic Texts*, presented by Henri de Lubac, trans. K. D. Whitehead (San Francisco: Ignatius, 1987) 30–32. See also de Lubac, "Yves de Montcheuil," in *Christian Resistance* 215–35.

119. Henri de Lubac, *At the Service of the Church: Henri de Lubac Reflects on the Circumstances That Occasioned His Writings*, trans. Anne Elizabeth Englund (San Francisco: Ignatius, 1993) 55.

120. Milbank, *Suspended Middle* 3.

121. Henri de Lubac, S.J., *The Drama of Atheist Humanism* (San Francisco: Ignatius, (1995; orig. publ. 1949) 14.

122. Ibid. 24.

123. Ibid. 80.

124. Ibid. 91, 92.

125. Ibid. 489.

126. De Lubac, *At the Service of the Church* 67; for the "Fourvière affair," see 67–92.

127. See, e.g., Thomas O'Meara, "'Raid on the Dominicans': The Repression of 1954," *America* (5 February 1994) 8–16.

128. De Lubac, *At the Service of the Church* 64.

129. Schindler, "Introduction" xxii n. 33; De Lubac, *At the Service of the Church* 308–9; Henri de Lubac, *Theology in History*, trans. Anne Englund Nash (San Francisco: Ignatius, 1996) 281–82.

130. De Lubac, *Drama of Atheist Humanism* 95–111. The title quotes Søren Kierkegaard's *Post-scriptum*: "Preparation for becoming attentive to Christianity does not consist in reading books or in making surveys of world history, but in *deeper immersion in existence*" (ibid. 111).

131. Ibid.

132. Karl Rahner, "Christian Pessimism," in *Theological Investigations* 22, trans. Joseph Donceel (New York: Crossroad, 1991) 155–62. See also Paul G. Crowley, "Rahner's Christian Pessimism: A Response to the Sorrow of AIDS," *Theological Studies* 58 (1997) 286–307.

133. Herbert Vorgrimler, *Understanding Karl Rahner: An Introduction to His Life and Thought*, trans. John Bowden (New York: Crossroad, 1986) 58–62, at 59.

134. Ibid. 68–70.

135. Mary Frances Coady, *With Bound Hands: A Jesuit in Nazi Germany. The Life and Selected Prison Letters of Alfred Delp* (Chicago: Loyola, 2003) 10, 23–24; Rahner, quoted in Harvey D. Egan, S.J., *Karl Rahner: The Mystic of Everyday Life* (New York: Crossroad, 1998) 22. See also Alan C. Mitchell, "Biographical Preface," in *Alfred Delp, S.J.: Prison Writings*, intro. Thomas Merton (Maryknoll, N.Y.: Orbis, 2004; orig. publ. 1963) vii–xix.

136. Vorgrimler, *Understanding Karl Rahner* 92.

137. Letter of Karl Rahner to Herbert Vorgimler (June 26, 1962), in ibid. 149–51, at 150.

138. Ibid. 92–101; quotation from Carolus Balić, O.F.M., at 99.

139. Collected as Karl Rahner, *The Need and the Blessing of Prayer*, trans. Bruce W. Gillette (Collegeville, Minn.: Liturgical, 1997).

140. Lothar Kettenacker, ed., *Ein Volk von Opfern? Die neue Debatte um den Bombenkrieg, 1940–45* (Berlin: Rowohlt, 2003); Jörg Friedrich, *Der Brand: Deutschland im Bombenkrieg 1940–1945* (Berlin: Propyläen, 2002).

141. Rahner, *Need and Blessing* 3.

142. Ibid.

143. Ibid. 6, 7.

144. Ibid. 8, 12.

145. Ibid. 15, 20, 45.

146. Hurley, quoted in Rynne, *History of Vatican II* 349; Rahner, quoted in Schloesser, *Jazz Age Catholicism* 3. See Karl Rahner, *Nature and Grace: Dilemmas in the Modern Church* (New York: Sheed & Ward, 1963; orig. publ. 1950).

147. Vorgrimler, *Understanding Karl Rahner* 3.
148. Alvin Toffler, *Future Shock* (New York: Random House, 1970).
149. Ernest Becker, *The Denial of Death* (New York: Free Press, 1973).
150. Chadwick, *Secularization* 48–139.
151. Rahner, *Need and Blessing* 46, 47.

4.

"THE TIMES THEY ARE A-CHANGIN'": A RESPONSE TO O'MALLEY AND SCHLOESSER

Neil J. Ormerod

Inspired by two recent articles in this journal regarding the fact and nature of change at Vatican II, this article analyzes the nature of this change. Drawing on the author's previous writings on ecclesiology and the social sciences, it argues that Vatican II was necessary to restore integrity to the mission of the Roman Catholic Church to the world.

> In a higher world it is otherwise;
> but here below to live is to change,
> and to be perfect is to change often.
> —John Henry Newman[1]

JOHN O'MALLEY'S PROVOCATIVE ARTICLE, "Vatican II: Did Anything Happen?"[2] and the enthralling response by Stephen Schloesser, "Against Forgetting: Memory, History, Vatican II,"[3] present us with a profound historical analysis of the context and documents of the Second Vatican Council. Both are exemplary works in their fundamental discipline of church history. In light of continuing disagreement over the "basic interpretation" of the council, of questions of continuity and discontinuity, O'Malley raises the question, "Did anything happen at Vatican II? Anything of significance?"[4] He identifies one school of thought that so stresses the continuity of the council with the tradition as to suggest that nothing really significant happened at all.[5] He argues strongly that something significant in fact did happen, focusing our attention in particular on the shift in the literary genre of the conciliar documents and the significance of that shift for the life of the Catholic Church. Schloesser affirms O'Malley's basic insight about *"how* the council, while keeping faith with tradition, also broke with the past. . . . And yet," Schloesser continues, "seeing *how* the council did this has made me wonder only more insistently *why* such a rupture was not only conceivable but necessary."[6] He then goes on to provide examples of the major social and cultural forces operating prior to and during the council that necessitated its changes. Both authors strongly affirm the reality of change arising from the council. Something did happen, and indeed something had to happen, for the good of the Church.

I do not intend to take issue with any of the arguments or conclusions of these two articles. Rather, I want to take them as a starting point for further reflections. In a number of publications I have argued, following the lead of Joseph Komonchak and Robert Doran, for the need to develop a historical ecclesiology grounded in a systematics of history.[7] Komonchak's work has been foundational for the considerations of my article. In a collection of essays published under the title, *Foundations in Ecclesiology*, Komonchak spells out a program for the revisioning of ecclesiology as concretely history and as requiring a thorough engagement with the social sciences.[8] Drawing on the writings of Bernard Lonergan, Komonchak's work is foundational and programmatic, and its implementation would of necessity be one of collaboration, for no single scholar could hope to master all aspects that are required. Of the many riches to be found in this work I focus on three.

First, ecclesiology is concerned with the concrete history of the Church, or what Komonchak often refers to as the "concrete self-realizations of the Church."[9] The object of ecclesiological study "is not only _what is said_ about the Church in the New Testament, in the apostolic Symbol, in the liturgy, in descriptions of ministry, but also _what was coming to be_ as the Church in the formation and reception of all four elements."[10] Ecclesiology must resist the temptation to focus on texts and documents that speak about the Church; it must rather focus on the Church itself. This is a much richer field of data that incorporates persons, their actions and decisions, the emergence of movements and institutions, the shifts in ecclesial cultures (which texts and document may signify), as well as the realization (and failures) of the redemptive mission of the Church throughout history.

Second, ecclesiology must engage with the social sciences. Komonchak argues that, "just as one cannot construct a theology without an at least implicit philosophy, so one cannot construct an ecclesiology without an implicit social theory; and without making the implicit explicit and securing its foundations neither construction can be considered critical."[11] Coming to grips with social theory is necessary if theology is to move beyond description into explanation, beyond common sense and into a realm of theory. The Church is a social and historical reality, so it is essential to a systematic understanding of the Church to employ tools developed for a systematic understanding of social and historical realities. "How can one work out a systematic ecclesiology without working out first such terms as 'individual,' 'community,' 'society,' 'meaning,' 'change,' 'structure,' 'institution,' 'relationship,' and so on, and the various relationships, or at least types of relationships, that can obtain among these those terms?"[12] Komonchak is aware of the difficulties involved, in particular "the ecclesiologist who attempts it will not find himself before a unified body of social theory,"[13] though he is less explicit on the theological dimension of social theory itself.[14]

Third, Komonchak places ecclesiology within a larger field of a theology of history. The Church as a redemptive process of self-constitution is a historical realization of the twin missions of the Word and Spirit.[15] These divine missions are constitutive of the redemptive intent of God in human history. The history of the Church is a moment in the larger history of humanity, and so ecclesiology finds its natural home in a larger theology of history itself. As I note below, significant advances in the development of a larger theology of history can be found in the work of Robert Doran.[16]

To further such a project requires active engagement with and reorientation of the social sciences.[17] In this article I want to present how the results of these two articles might appear within the type of project I am envisaging. In doing so I wish to illustrate that, while the two articles make for excellent church history, they do not theologically analyze the material considered.[18] A historical ecclesiology is not just a historical narrative of the Church. It "should be empirical/historical, critical, normative, dialectic and practical."[19]

As I have noted above, the O'Malley and Schloesser articles both focus on the fact of change in the Catholic Church as a result of Vatican II. Change is something that the Church has always found difficult to account for and acknowledge. As Ben Meyer noted of the early church, "they did not *acknowledge* development. They overlooked it. They suppressed its novelty, intent on ways of relocating the creative aspects of their own historical experience, safely and objectively, in God's eschatological saving act."[20] And, one might well argue, so it has been ever since. As O'Malley notes, "the Church is by definition a conservative society."[21] This is not merely a sociological observation; it is a theological necessity, given the Church's foundation in the historical events of Jesus' life, death, and resurrection. While Schloesser identifies an implicit anxiety in the documents of Vatican II about "fragmentation and disunity,"[22] there has also been a constant anxiety about change itself.

This anxiety about change finds theological expression in a type of idealistic ecclesiology that takes the Church out of history and places it in some ideal realm. Whether it be the "perfect society" ecclesiology of Robert Bellarmine, the "mystical body of Christ" ecclesiology of Pius XII, or the *communio* ecclesiologies of more recent times, they are characterized by their lack of interest in historical details and events. They present a timeless, unchanging church, often a very attractive church, but one disconnected from any actual historical community. In contrast to this style of ecclesiology there are a growing number of ecclesiologies that take historical data seriously and hence must come to terms with the reality of historical change.[23] Walter Kasper has characterized the distinction between these two approaches as one between a Platonic and an Aristotelian theology: "The conflict is between theological opinions and underlying philosophical assumptions. One side proceeds by Plato's method; its starting point is the primacy of an ideal that is a universal concept. The other side follows Aristotle's approach and sees the universal as existing in a concrete reality."[24]

While one side is deeply suspicious of change, which can only mean a movement away from an ideal state, the other side takes change for granted. As change is a key issue in this division, this is where I begin my investigation.

The Question of Change

Change is a complex notion, particularly when one is dealing with historical communities such as the Church. At present, for example, there is considerable debate about the issue of globalization. Is it a reality? What is driving it? Is it primarily economic, political, or cultural? Where is it taking us? When we look at the Church, it is obvious that some things have changed. The priest now faces the people; the liturgy is in the vernacular; the pope travels by jet airplane, and the Vatican has a web site. Such changes are obvious and undeniable. Clearly, those who want to minimize claims to change are not suggesting that these changes have not occurred. Perhaps they want to suggest that nothing essential has changed, but then that suggestion simply opens up questions about what is essential and what is accidental, with all the attendant difficulties of essentialist thinking.

In fact, understanding change is a key issue in any study of human communities. In his often noted but as yet unpublished "File 713—History," Bernard Lonergan sought to develop elements for a *summa sociologica* that would "throw Hegel and Marx, despite the enormity of their influence on this very account, into the shade."[25] While perusing this file some ten years ago, a cryptic throwaway line caught my eye: "constants disappear when you differentiate." Here Lonergan was drawing an analogy between the task of a social theory and Newton's first law of motion. Newton's key insight was that constant motion needed no explanation—bodies at constant velocity continued in that motion unless acted upon by an external force.[26] Lonergan was suggesting something similar in the field of the social sciences. Human communities are complex realities that aim to some extent at "self-reproduction." Constancy in human communities does not as such require explanation. What requires explanation and analysis is change. Central to Lonergan's account of history was an analogy drawn from Newton's account of planetary motion. It consists of a series of three approximations. In the first, the ideal line of history, people "always do what is intelligent and reasonable," resulting in pure progress. In the second, one grasps the presence of the unintelligible, unintelligent surd in human affairs, whereby people are unintelligent and unreasonable in their decisions, and these result in decline. In the third, there is renaissance or redemption that by God's grace moves humanity closer to the ideal line of history, of pure progress. In its own way this basic heuristic structure reappears throughout Lonergan's career, certainly in *Insight* and in *Method in Theology*, but also in various occasional pieces as well. The most significant of these is the essay, "Healing and Creating in History."[27] This essay is a sophisticated transposition of the classical grace-nature distinction into social and historical categories.

Robert Doran has built on Lonergan's proposals, developing his notion of a hierarchical scale of values—vital, social, cultural, personal, and religious—by identifying dialectic structures of transcendence and limitation at the social, cultural, and personal levels. These, together with Lonergan's notion of healing and creating in history, provide a heuristic structure for ordering history: "Taken together these three processes constitute . . . the immanent intelligibility of the process of human history. . . . History is to be conceived as a complex network of dialectics of subjects, communities and cultures. Insofar as these dialectics are integral, history is intelligible. Insofar as these dialectics are distorted, history is a compound of the intelligible and the surd."[28] In a more recent work, Doran adds to these elements four created communications of the divine nature corresponding to the four trinitarian relations, to develop what he calls a "unified field theory" for a systematic theology of history.[29]

Four points should be noted about Doran's proposal, built on Lonergan's foundations. First, the structure is thoroughly dynamic. Lonergan's three overarching categories of progress, decline, and redemption are all categories of change. The dialectic structures Doran develops at the personal, cultural, and social levels are elements that produce personal, cultural, and social change. There are creative movements up the scale of values and healing movements down the scale. The structure incorporates integrative forces that seek to maintain stability but also operative forces that move in the direction of self-transcendence. Change is built in from the start.

Second, the structure is normative. The normative force of Lonergan's transcendental precepts operates at all levels of the structure. The social order arises as a normative response to practical intelligence seeking recurrent solutions to the need for the production and just and equitable distribution of vital values. The cultural order arises as a normative response of the human need to find meaning and purpose in daily living. The personal order is our own normative orientation to meaning, truth, and goodness, which enables us to move beyond our social and cultural context and beyond mere personal satisfaction, to ask about the truly good that is yet to be achieved. The dialectics at the personal, cultural, and social levels identify a normative order of self-transcendence, an operator that relentlessly transforms all our current settled situations.

Third, the structure is dialectical. It recognizes not merely the normative order of self-transcendence, but also the real and indeed realized possibility of historical decline. Lonergan speaks of the shorter and longer cycles of decline, while Doran analyzes the potential breakdowns in the personal, cultural, and social dialectics. These patterns of breakdown and decline provide a rich set of conceptual tools for analyzing particular historical situations and the problems they embody.

Fourth, the structure is both thoroughly "social scientific" and theological. It recognizes the autonomy of the social, cultural, and personal levels, but only as a relative autonomy. The social is open to the cultural, the cultural to the personal, and the personal is ultimately open to the possibility of grace. The healing vector of grace initiates religious conversion, then moral conversion (personal level), and in some cases intellectual conversion (cultural level). Moral conversion raises questions of social justice and equity (social level) and so transforms societies "from above." As such, the structure rejects the conceptualist assumptions of methods of correlation that tend to disconnect the sociocultural from the religious as separate realms or spheres, only then to have difficulty in reconnecting them in any meaningful way.[30]

Trajectories of Change

If the issue is one of change, what then does the structure developed by Lonergan and Doran tell us about change? What are the major trajectories of change that will provide us with a heuristic structure for analyzing what happened not only at Vatican II, but at any other major historical event? In seeking to respond to this question, I focus on the social and cultural levels of the scale of values as most relevant to the problem of historical change. I take Lonergan's notion of healing and creative vectors and generalize it to movements from "below up" and "above down." Some of what I have already written on this matter in an earlier article I repeat here.[31]

Trajectory 1: From Practical Insight to Cultural Change

The trajectory begins with a new practical insight that alters the social situation. This insight may be a new technological development—for example, the invention of computers; or a new economic insight such as the free market; or a new political insight such as representative democracy. If the practical insight works, that is, if it increases the flow of basic goods, improves the efficiency of the distribution of those goods, or increases the sense of belonging in society on a recurrent basis, then it will lead to the development of lasting institutions that embody this practicality. This practical insight will in turn lead to new meanings and values that incorporate it as part of the social story, the new social identity, and the way things should be done. Thus, the cultural superstructure may respond to developments in the social infrastructure by incorporating new meanings and values consonant with the social change. A conflict-ualist sociology invariably understands such a process as ideological, but it need not be thought as such.[32] Meaning-making is essential for fully human living—human beings do not live by bread alone—and while meaning may occasionally be distorted, without it our lives would be subhuman. This meaning-making may, however, be ideological, if the practical insight neglects other communal values, and if the meanings and values that arise justify that neglect by denying the validity of those communal values. Thus, with liberation theology and critical theory, we must ask, Who are the victims of this social change? Who is marginalized? Whose voice has not been heard? We must ask whether the practical insight suffers from bias, either individual, group, or general. All these are possibilities. But in the ideal shift, new practical insights give rise to cultural shifts that, recognizing their own contingency, can avoid ideological pretensions and distortions. Culture is then a creative, contingent, indeed artistic expression of the human spirit helping us make sense of our social world. We arrive at a new, relatively stable social and cultural state that incorporates the shift brought about by practical intelligence.

Trajectory 2: From Cultural Change to Practical Insight

The second trajectory begins with the emergence of new meanings and values. How can this happen? It can occur when one culture comes into contact with another, as when European culture "discovered" the East and developed new art; or when Islamic scholars brought Aristotle to the Christian Middle Ages. It can happen when a creative person develops a new philosophy or even a new religion. Most significantly, it can occur when God communicates new meanings and values in human history through revelation. This revelation is most evident in the incarnate meaning of the person of Jesus Christ, his life, death, and resurrection. It is then further carried in the hearts and minds of his followers, particularly the saints. It finds written expression in the Scriptures and definitive judgment in the dogmas of the church and the writings of theologians. Whatever their source, new meanings and values may be incompatible with the present social ordering. New insights into the meaning of human dignity may be incompatible with slavery, the denial of women's voting rights, and child labor. These insights grow among people through debate, discussion, and art. Cultural institutions are formed to promote a certain vision of life around these new meanings and values. People begin to envisage a new social ordering through a multiplicity of practical insights more expressive of the emerging meanings and values that give purpose to their lives. These new emerging meanings may of course represent the biased interests of a particular group. They may reflect a distorted meaning such as racism. But they may also represent a greater attunement to the intentional goals of truth, goodness, and beauty. Such an attunement will lead to a healing of distortions in the social order.

I would now like to supplement this basic proposal by bringing it into dialogue with Christopher Dawson's identification of five "main types of social change."[33] The merit of Dawson's proposal is that it has emerged not from theoretical *a priori* consideration as above, but *a posteriori*, on the basis of his historical investigations. However, I change the order of his presentation to suit the current context.

Case 1: "The simple case of a people that develops its way of life in its original environment without the intrusion of human factors from outside."[34] This is a case of relative stability in which the two trajectories outlined above move a society incrementally forward.

Case 2: "The case of a people which comes into a new geographical environment and readapts its culture as a consequence."[35] A new geographical environment demands new practical insights to meet the needs of survival. Inevitably these insights have an impact on the culture of the group. New stories must be told, new cosmologies developed, even new theologies. This case is an example of Trajectory 1.

Case 3: "The case of a people that adopts some element of material culture which has been developed by another people elsewhere."[36] Dawson notes how rapidly elements of material culture can move from one society to another, instancing the spread of the use of metals, of agriculture, and irrigation in the ancient world.

However, he adds, "it is remarkable how often such external change leads not to social progress, but to social decay."[37] This again is an example of Trajectory 1, where a practical insight has been borrowed from others. Dawson's observation about the possible negative impact perhaps reflects instances where the disparity between the two levels of technology is such as to cause a fundamental collapse of the world of meaning of the recipient society.

Case 4: "The case of a people which modifies its way of life owing to the adoption of new knowledge or belief, or to some change in its view of life and its conception of reality."[38] The way Dawson puts this makes it clear that this "new knowledge" is not just a new technique or product of practical intelligence—what he previously referred to as "some element of material culture." Dawson is indicating a major cultural shift, a new "conception of reality." The source of this new conception is "Reason" or the "mind of man."[39] This case is clearly an example of Trajectory 2.

Case 5: "The case of two different peoples, each with its own way of life and social organization, which mix with one another usually as the result of conquest, occasionally as a result of peaceful contact." Dawson describes cultural mixing as "the most typical and important of all causes of cultural change." [40] It is clearly also the most complex, as it involves elements of all the above types, movements "across" as well as "up and down." There are exchanges at the level of practical intelligence and at the realm of meanings and values. New forms of intersubjective identification must develop, as well as new stories, myths, philosophies, and theologies to accommodate the new context. Dawson speaks of this case as initiating a "period of intense cultural activity, when new forms of life created by the vital union of two different peoples and cultures burst into flower." [41] He warns that it can also result in "violent conflicts and revolts of spasmodic action, and brilliant promise that has no fulfillment."[42]

While Case 5 is complex, there is a certain sense in which the previous four cases constitute components within it. Moreover, each case is greatly clarified by bringing it into dialogue with the perspective of the two trajectories draw from Lonergan and Doran. Taken together the two trajectories and five cases provide a good set of heuristic tools for an analysis of major social and cultural change.

In the light of our present discussion, we may ask not just *how* change happened (O'Malley) or *why* it happened (Schloesser), but "what *type* of change happened at Vatican II?"

Vatican II: What Happened?

To assess what type of change happened at Vatican II, one must first have an account of the situation prior to the event.[43] Such an account must not simply identify the historical conditions antecedent to the council, but must also provide an analytic framework for understanding this cluster of conditions. Both O'Malley and Schloesser use Lonergan's notion of a transition from classicism to historical consciousness to provide some understanding of the nature of the Church's prior situation.[44] The Church had locked itself into a classicist understanding of culture as a normative ideal that it possessed and others must attain. This stance is certainly evident in the Church's missionary endeavors that were as much about planting European culture as they were about preaching the gospel.[45] As Schloesser notes, this stance had a particularly negative impact on the Church's missionary endeavors in Asia. I would now like to make this account of the Church prior to Vatican II more explanatory by drawing on Doran's notions of the dialectics at the cultural and social levels of value.

As noted above, these notions are conceived as dialectics of transcendence and limitation. The normativity of the structure dictates that these two poles be held in dialectic tension, while recognizing the priority of the transforming power of the transcendent pole of the dialectic. A breakdown of the dialectic occurs when a community moves in one direction of the dialectic or the other, to the neglect or even rejection of the opposing pole. Given the two dialectics at the two levels, there are four distinctive antitypes or patterns of breakdown in the sociocultural context of any community. I have analyzed this typology elsewhere; here I draw attention to what I call the classic conservative antitype.[46]

Classic Conservative Antitype

The classic conservative antitype represents a distortion of both the cultural and social dialectic in the direction of limitation. At the cultural level there is a strong emphasis on tradition. The past is normative, not as a prototype for future development, but as an archetype to be endlessly repeated. The tradition sets the standard for theology, philosophy, art, literature, and so on. Any innovations at the cultural level, such as new theologies or new philosophies, are seen as a threat to the purity of the tradition. This distortion of the cultural dialectic in the direction of limitation can go hand in hand with a strong sense of transcendence, but there is a compensatory distortion in the way such transcendence is conceived. Because the culture is not in touch with the reality of actual cultural self-transcendence, it may conceive of transcendence in some purely "spiritual" sense, as in an extrinsicist account of grace, or some other "other-worldly" understanding of religion.

At the social level a rigidity of social organization is present. The distortion toward limitation does not mean a lack of social organization. Rather this distortion implies the inability of that organization to adapt to changing social circumstances with new solutions arising from practical intelligence. Instead, problems are met with a reliance on old "tried and true" methods. Such groups have a strong sense of community and social identity. There can be genuine experiences of warmth and fellowship. However, the distortion of the dialectic in the direction of limitation can mean that the intersubjective warmth can be perverted into shared anxieties or psychotic fantasies, particularly those of a strong leader. Again there is a compensatory distortion of how social transcendence is conceived. Rather than being seen in terms of practical intelligence resolving new problems through new social structures, it may be seen more in terms of "growth," that is, becoming a bigger group. Mission then means "others joining our group."

The coherence between the two distortions, both being in the direction of limitation, means that such communities are highly resistant to change and strongly successful in self-reproduction. There is a tendency to see the world in hostile terms; hence, one must separate oneself from the world. This antitype corresponds, perhaps, to the sociological understanding of a sect.[47] As a breakdown in the integrity of the social and cultural dialectics, this typology is not just an analytic category; it represents a failure of a church community to effectively realize its mission.

It is not difficult to mount a case that prior to Vatican II the Catholic Church approximated such an antitype. In the wake of the Reformation the Catholic Church adopted a defensive attitude toward its ecclesial opponents. This defensiveness spread to emerging sciences, political changes, philosophical approaches, and eventually to the whole of modern society. It found its peak expression in Pius IX's Syllabus of Errors.[48] The Church defined itself by its rejection of the modern world. Theologically the era was marked by an increasing extrinsicism that separated grace from nature and viewed the spiritual life as one cut off from the world.[49] The mission of the Church was conceived as "saving souls," focusing on the beatific vision, but not so much on the resurrection of the body.[50] Socially the Church presented itself as strongly cohesive, but it expressed its chronic anxiety about the "other" through its scapegoating treatment of the Jewish people.[51] Its social forms of organization displayed remarkable persistence through the centuries from Trent to the 20th century.[52] Overall the Church displayed remarkable stability to the point of being static, resistant to the forces that were effectively reshaping the world. Indeed, it even made a virtue of this stability, stressing its unchanging nature.

As I noted earlier, this type of community is highly resistant to change. It does not allow for human creativity to operate either at the social level of organization and practicality, or at the cultural level of philosophy, theology, and critical reflection. The community of the Church represented a relatively self-enclosed subcommunity of the larger society. It is likely that in such a community change can occur only where it is sanctioned and even initiated "from above." Even so, such a community will face change with considerable resistance because of its long-term commitments to suppress novelty. On the other hand, an increasing disconnectedness between the Church and the world creates great tension between its members who must live both "in" the Church and "in" the world.

In this situation it seems appropriate to compare the change initiated in the Church at Vatican II to that of the fifth case considered above. The change was not a simple shift at the level of practicality or of culture. Rather, it was a complex interaction at the social and cultural levels, the conditions for the possibility of which had been established by centuries of separation from, and resistance to, the changes taking place in the world. In such circumstances it is not unusual that the council initiated a "period of intense cultural activity, when new forms of life created by the vital union of two different peoples and cultures burst into flower" but also the possibility of "violent conflicts and revolts of spasmodic action, and brilliant promise that has no fulfillment."[53] Indeed Dawson's words here have a prophetic character in relation to the aftermath of Vatican II. It has been a period of intense cultural activity, but also a period of increasing conflict over the basic interpretation of the council, leading some to fear that the initial brilliant promise of the council has not been fulfilled.

A Missiological Imperative to Change

As I already suggested, a church that approximates the classic conservative antitype represents a community that effectively fails to realize its mission. This assertion is full of theological judgments that need unpacking. As I have suggested in a previous article, the Church is defined teleologically, that is, by its mission.[54] In contemporary writings that mission is expressed heuristically by the symbol of the kingdom of God. The mission of the Church involves the building of God's kingdom. Nonetheless this mission is not exclusive to the Church. As John Paul II put it: "The kingdom is the concern of everyone: individuals, society, and the world. Working for the kingdom means acknowledging and promoting God's activity, which is present in human history and transforms it. *Building the kingdom means working for liberation from evil in all its forms.* In a word, the kingdom of God is the manifestation and the realization of God's plan of salvation in all its fullness."[55]

Now if the antitypes represent a breakdown in the integral dialectics of the scale of values, if such breakdown represents a movement away from the ideal path of progress and into the path of decline, then they are a manifestation of social and cultural evil, which Lonergan refers to as the social surd. The Church does not and cannot contribute to working for the kingdom by manifesting evil in its own life and operations. The Church therefore has a missiological imperative to change.

This missiological understanding of the Church is evident in the opening paragraph of *Lumen gentium*: "Since the Church is in Christ like a sacrament or as a sign and instrument both of a very closely knit union with God and of the unity of the whole human race, it desires now to unfold more fully to the faithful of the Church and to the whole world its own inner nature and universal mission." It is reaffirmed in the opening paragraph of *Gaudium et spes*: "United in Christ, they are led by the Holy Spirit in their journey to the Kingdom of their Father and they have welcomed the news of salvation which is meant for every man. That is why this community realizes that it is truly linked with mankind and its history by the deepest of bonds." The Church has a universal mission, a mission of salvation, as a sign and instrument of the unity of the whole human race and its history. The Church's mission has an essentially historical dimension. Because the world changes, because each new age brings new problems and challenges, the Church must find new ways to deal with these new problems and challenges. In short, it must change to fulfill its mission in a changing world.

Schloesser has identified one aspect of the missiological failure of the pre-Vatican II Church. He notes Archbishop Giovanni Benelli's statement of 1973: "There is no doubt that in the Middle Ages and subsequently up to twenty years ago, there was in the Church a centralization of powers" that had "contributed to delaying for centuries the conversion of Asia."[56] And no doubt the evangelizing mission of the Church in Asia has met with significant resistance. However, a far greater failure of the Church's mission can be identified much closer to home. Western Europe is increasingly post-Christian. With the Enlightenment and the scientific revolution, Catholicism increasingly lost the intellectual class. With the industrial revolution, it increasingly lost the workers. With the rise of democracy and the emergence of the modern secular state, it lost any privileged political position and has become increasingly irrelevant to the middle classes. The seeds of this failure were laid in the increasingly sectlike characteristics of the Catholic Church itself. Its hostility to the changes taking place in the modern world presented the Western world with too stark an option, of either Catholic Christianity or modernity. A failure to recognize the more positive aspects of modernity and to embrace these has left the Church increasingly out in the cold.

The Church has recognized some of its failure in Western Europe with the calls of both John Paul II and Benedict XVI for a reevangelization of Europe, and for Europe to reaffirm its Christian roots. These are certainly important goals. But on the present analysis, if these goals mean simply that Europe must come back to the Church and a form of Christianity that existed in the past, without any significant shift in the Church itself, reevangelization will fail. As John Allen notes in his review of George Weigel's, *Witness to Hope: A Biography of John Paul II*: "Delegates at the Dialogue for Austria [Salzburg, 1998] repeatedly stressed that for John Paul's new evangelization to work, the church first must get its internal house in order. As long as Europeans—or anyone else—perceive the church as an oppressor of women, gays and dissidents, it is unlikely to generate much sympathetic attention."[57]

A Mission to the World

This recognition of the need for change, of course, is not to give a blanket endorsement of the modern world, as if the Church should simply conform itself to the world without critique. Far from it. One may argue that just as the Church has suffered distortion because of its rejection of major currents in modernity, so too the world, or at least the Western world, has suffered distortion because of its separation from the Church. Just as both the social and cultural dialectics identified by Doran can be distorted in the direction of limitation, leading to a context that actively resists both social and cultural change, so too can they be distorted in the direction of transcendence.

Totally Progressive Antitype

The totally progressive antitype represents a distortion of the cultural dialectic and the social dialectic in the direction of transcendence.

At a cultural level such communities embrace new ideas, new theologies, new philosophies, and new worldviews very quickly, since they are not held back by the past. Rather than see the past as authoritative, they tend to view the past with suspicion, sharing the Enlightenment's "prejudice against prejudice." In a form of intellectual evolutionary optimism, the new idea is seen as inevitably better. However, because such groups are no longer grounded in an intellectual tradition, they lack the ability to discriminate between cultural progress and cultural decline. They fail to recognize the traditional character of all cultures, including the one to which they belong, a point Alasdair MacIntyre emphasizes.[58] As a consequence there is a tendency to be intellectually faddish and superficial.

At the social level there is a willingness to adapt to new situations, to make use of new technologies in communication, and to move away from methods that worked in the past but have lost their appeal. While such communities may generate excitement and a sense of immediate togetherness, the distortion in the direction of practical intelligence may lead to undervaluing intersubjectivity beyond a superficial level, for they fail to recognize that the affective bonds of genuine community are cross-generational and may reach back for decades, even centuries. Such communities may lack a stable social identity, and there may be a high level of mobility within them. The neglect of intersubjectivity means that their members do not produce enduring communities, but exhibit significant geographical mobility. Moreover, the distortion in the direction of practical intelligence may lead to a faddish adoption of new social techniques, programs, and technologies, with little critical appreciation of longer-term affects on the community as a whole.

Again, these two distortions are mutually reinforcing, though the outcomes will be very different from those of the classic conservative antitype. These groups take on new ideas and new social processes on a regular basis. At an extreme, the only form of social organization is what is required to meet an immediate practical need. The basic form of gathering is the workshop, the seminar, or the conference called to impart the latest new idea or teaching. The intellectual and social identity of such groups is short-lived as people and ideas come and go in a constant turnover. They provide a brief and intense experience of sharing, but it is generally superficial with no enduring sense of community. They exhibit an intellectual syncretism and a fragmented social organization. Significantly, they may have a compensatory bias toward cosmological symbolism, which represents the limitation pole of the cultural dialectic.[59] There may also be a tendency to idealize more traditional communal forms, while providing little hope of ever truly attaining such forms.

Again, as with the description of the Church prior to Vatican II in terms of the classic conservative antitype, it is not difficult to mount a case that our modern world suffers from the distortion evident in this totally progressive antitype. Certainly the practical intelligence of neoliberal economic theory is dominating the West, effectively silencing voices that speak of social capital or community values. Technology is all-pervasive, and the pace of technological change shows no sign of slowing. Our ethical reflections are playing catch-up, particularly in areas of biotechnology. Our political and legal institutions too are playing catch-up in a world trapped in the ever-increasing demands of a globalizing economy. Culturally we are caught up in a postmodern relativism that undercuts all claims to traditional authority and truth. In the face of rapid social and cultural change, a protest movement of "tribalization" occurs that reasserts the values of local communities and their cultures.[60]

Of course, one does not want to oversimplify our present context. Cultures and social structures are pluriform; in particular, a culture will empirically consist of dominant and subversive voices, loud and soft voices, affirmative and protesting voices. The totally progressive antitype is just a type, not realized in any human community in its "pure" form. Nonetheless, it is suggestive of the situation of decline, or of distortion, evident in the social and cultural dialectics in our present context.

To the extent that this analysis is accurate, it suggests that the failure of the Church's mission has been a failure to mediate the healing vector of salvation to our present historical context. While the world has moved in one direction of distortion, the Church has moved reactively in the other. Both have suffered as a result. However, these mutually opposed movements of Church and world away from the integrity of the social and cultural dialectics created the conditions for the possibility of the type of interaction proposed by Dawson between two distinct communities. In the short term this interaction has had more impact on the Church because it has moved from a more static to a more dynamic state. Moreover, these changes occurred simultaneously at the level of both social organization and culture. These changes impacted the organizational processes of parishes and dioceses, with, for example, the adoption of pastoral councils, finance committees, and new liturgical forms, as well as new theologies and philosophies at the cultural level. In the shorter and longer term, the Church's success in bringing the distortions of our present culture back toward some form of dialectic balance remains an open question. Certainly, much of the Church's social teaching is a resource for those who want to argue for a realignment of our present social and cultural dialectics.[61]

Empirical, Critical, Normative, Dialectical, and *Practical*

The claim of my proposal in relation to ecclesiology is that it should be based on an empirical and critical analysis of the historical data, the adoption of a normative framework, and a dialectic account of the breakdown from that normativity, together with a practical therapeutic based on that account. Now is the time to identify some elements of that therapeutic. Since this is an article in ecclesiology, I focus on the situation of the Church and leave the situation of the world to the larger concern of missiology.[62]

While Vatican II was surely not the sole agent of change in the Church's life,[63] it was the major source of sanction for the process of change that has occurred. Given the Church's approximation to the classic conservative antitype, for any movement of change to be successful, it needed sanctioning from the top. The council provided that sanction, with the oft-noted notion of the "spirit of Vatican II" being used repeatedly to justify elements of change in the life of the Church. Nonetheless it needs to be acknowledged that, overall, the process of change was not well managed. No one was prepared for the pace of change that occurred after the council, certainly not the people in the pews. Largely practical changes in the liturgy and other sacramental practices were in place within just a few years of the council. Previously hidden topics such as the ordination of married men, and even of women, were openly discussed. Were these just matters of practicality, or were there genuine theological reasons involved? Theology itself departed from its neo-Scholastic bindings and experimented with other philosophical approaches, while the impact of critical historical studies in the Bible began to be felt. Once the genie of change was released from its bottle, it would be difficult to put it back in. What then were the limits and the possibilities involved in the process?

The decades after the council have reflected this struggle to identify limits and explore possibilities. Under the direction of Cardinal Joseph Ratzinger, the Congregation for the Doctrine of the Faith made a number of strategic interventions in areas of moral theology, Christology, liberation theology, ecclesiology, and the theology of religious pluralism.[64] In the curious mix of the cultural and the practical that we call liturgy, the Vatican also acted to eliminate "liturgical experimentation" and reassert control of different aspects of the liturgy, the current struggle over English translation being but one example. At the practical level we have seen major reviews of canon law, of seminary and religious life, and so on. While the soundness of some of these might be questioned, they must be located against the background of the dynamic process that Vatican II sanctioned. Having sanctioned change, the Church then sought to define the parameters of that change, particularly at the cultural level, but also at the level of social organization.

The greatest dangers in this process are to be found among those who seek an undifferentiated return to the past, the dangers of integralism or restorationism. These forces need to be resisted, because they would represent a loss of nerve in the transforming mission of the Church to the world and a repetition of the mistakes of the past. As I noted above, the classic conservative antitype is highly resistant to change, and it is not difficult to identify persons and groups who represent such resistance within the Church. The most extreme version is that of the traditionalist followers of Archbishop Marcel Lefèbvre (1905–1991), who seem to reject completely the validity of Vatican II. However extreme they may be, over the long pontificate of John Paul II, representatives of such resistance to change seem to have gained notable support.

On the other hand, a danger remains, particularly at the cultural level, that theologians and other cultural agents will conform themselves to the "spirit of the age." Some seem to view postmodern relativism not as a problem to be confronted, but as a solution to be adopted with some relish. The totally progressive orientation of the globalizing world will inevitably lead to social fragmentation and intellectual faddism. The healing of the distortions of the social and cultural dialectic is a concern for the Church and for theologians whose task it is to mediate "between a cultural matrix and the significance and role of religion in that matrix."[65] A central issue for theologians in dealing with this question is, I believe, struggling with the issue of the permanent validity of the dogmatic decrees of the Church.[66] These are an enduring stumbling block to all postmodern relativistic claims.

Nonetheless the Church has a long history of dealing with such problems. This is why the problem of restorationism is a far greater danger. The forces of resistance to change are playing to past strengths and enjoy greater institutional power than those who seek to promote change. In this context the current rise of *communio* ecclesiologies should be noted. In earlier articles I have criticized this style of ecclesiology, and I repeat my concerns here. Symbolically the notion of *communio* has an integrative function. It stresses values of harmony and integration. Such a function resists change, because change introduces stresses into the community that threaten to disrupt communal harmony.[67] Thus, the recognition of communion ecclesiology by the 1985 Synod of Bishops as the central and fundamental idea of the documents of Vatican II was not just a theological stance; it can be read as an expression of anxiety over potentially disruptive forces of change within the Church.[68] This is why communion ecclesiology has been so rapidly adopted by more conservative bishops seeking to put a halt to forces of change. The theme was further taken up in the 1992 statement of the Congregation for the Doctrine of the Faith, Some Aspects of the Church as Communion.

I have argued that, at the very least, *communio* ecclesiology requires some balancing by an emphasis on the mission of the Church as defining its identity. It is significant, then, that, while the congregation's 1992 statement emphasizes *communio,* mentioning the mission of the Church only a few times, the *Instrumentum laboris* of the 2001 Synod of Bishops, The Bishop: Servant of the Gospel of Jesus Christ for the Hope of the World, presents a different picture. Along with repeated statements about the "Church as communion," ("communion" appears about 180 times), it also mentions the missionary nature of the Church (about 85 times). On 20 occasions the two notions are joined, noting, for example, that "Communion and mission enrich each other. The force of communion makes the Church grow in extension and depth. At the same time, mission makes communion grow, extending it outwards in concentric circles, until it reaches everyone. Indeed, the Church spreads into various cultures and introduces them to the Kingdom, so that what comes from God can return to him. For this reason, it has been said: 'Communion leads to mission, and mission itself to communion.'"[69] While *communio* emphasizes the integrative function of the life of the Church and adds "depth," mission is the transformative, operative function that moves the Church beyond its present realm of comfort into dialogue, debate, and mediation to the world. I would argue that a proper recovery of the Church's essentially missionary character[70] is needed to prevent the Church from slipping back into the classic conservative antitype from which it attempted to escape through Vatican II. It is simply overloading the language of *communio* to expect it to carry forward this missionary aspect. In this regard, those who promote *communio* ecclesiology could well take note of the 2001 Synod document that is far more balanced in placing these two aspects into conjunction without seeking to reduce one to the other.

Conclusion

The 1960s was a period of great change and of consciousness of change. To some extent the "spirit of the age" was captured by Bob Dylan's song, "The Times They Are A-Changin'." This was a song of protest against those who wanted to tie the world to the past. The youth wanted emancipation from the forces of tradition, of social and cultural conservatism. Perhaps naïvely we did not realize that forces of change were already reshaping the world and had been doing so for centuries. Now, 40 years later, our concern is not one of promoting change in the world, but of questioning its direction and pace. Where are we going, and are we simply moving too fast?

These same forces of change, which the Catholic Church had resisted for centuries, Vatican II released into the life of the Church. While the anti-Modernist measures represented a last-ditch effort by the hierarchy to resist change, Vatican II sanctioned efforts to change, and these have since had an irrevocable effect on its life. Theologically, the Church's resistance to change represented a failure in its missionary stance to the world. Its hostility to change was indiscriminate. The Church set its face against the world and thus no longer effectively mediated the healing vector needed to help keep the world "in balance." The Church is now faced with the need to bring about change in itself (*aggiornamento* and *ressourcement*)[71] while seeking to put the breaks on the pace of change in the world. This is a delicate balancing act. It would be easy for the Church to be captured by a romantic idealism that would identify the Church as a place of solidity and permanence in an ever-changing world. However, it would be a sectarian Church, one caught up in the classic conservative antitype. To favor a world-rejecting hostility would be an abrogation of the Church's mission to the world. This must not be allowed to happen.

Finally, this article attempted to illustrate a style of ecclesiology promoted by Joseph Komonchak and developed further by myself. Drawing on categories from Doran's theology of history, it seeks to consider the Church in its concrete historical manifestations. Here the historical material has largely been provided in the two articles by O'Malley and Schloesser, but these have been further processed by categories that are at once sociological and theological. The two antitypes are basically sociological categories—what Lonergan refers to as general categories. However, they take on a theological significance when they are placed in relation to the Church's theological mission to work "for liberation from evil in all its forms."[72] I hope that I have illustrated how fruitful this style of ecclesiology can be.[73]

Notes

1. John Henry Newman, *An Essay on the Development of Christian Doctrine* (New York: Longmans, Green, 1909) 40.
2. John W. O'Malley, "Vatican II: Did Anything Happen?" *Theological Studies* 67 (2006) 3–33; republished in this volume.
3. Stephen Schloesser, "Against Forgetting: Memory, History, Vatican II," *Theological Studies* 67 (2006) 275–319; republished in this volume.
4. O'Malley, "Vatican II" above at 57.
5. Specifically O'Malley, ibid. 52–54, mentions the book by Archbishop Agostino Marchetto, *Il concilio ecumenico Vaticano II: Contrappunto per la sua storia* (Vatican City: Libreria Editrice Vaticana, 2005) in which Marchetto attacks the "Bologna school" for its interpretation of the council as a point of rupture.
6. Schloesser, "Against Forgetting" above at 94.
7. Neil J. Ormerod, "System, History, and a Theology of Ministry," *Theological Studies* 61 (2000) 432–46; Ormerod, "The Structure of a Systematic Ecclesiology," *Theological Studies* 63 (2002) 3–30.
8. Joseph A. Komonchak, *Foundations in Ecclesiology,* supplementary issue of *Lonergan Workshop* 11, ed. Fred Lawrence (Boston: Boston College, 1995). See also Komonchak, "The Significance

of Vatican Council II for Ecclesiology," in *Gift of the Church*, ed. Peter Phan (Collegeville, Minn.: Liturgical, 2000) 69–92; and "Vatican II as an 'Event'" in the present volume.

9. E.g., Komonchak, *Foundations in Ecclesiology* 53.

10. Ibid. 49; see also 50, 67, 68.

11. Ibid. 64.

12. Ibid. 69–70.

13. Ibid. 73.

14. This lacuna is reflected in Komonchak's actual engagement with social sciences in particular ecclesiological themes. His tendency is to draw on highly reputable authors and theorists rather than engage with the social sciences as a whole and seek to reorient them (as Lonergan suggests).

15. Komonchak, *Foundations in Ecclesiology* 48.

16. Robert M. Doran, *Theology and the Dialectics of History* (Toronto: University of Toronto, 1990).

17. Neil J. Ormerod, "A Dialectic Engagement with the Social Sciences in an Ecclesiological Context," *Theological Studies* 66 (2005) 815–40.

18. This is not meant as a criticism of these articles in any way. It is simply to argue for a collaborative division of labor as envisaged in Bernard J. F. Lonergan, *Method in Theology* (New York: Seabury, 1971).

19. Ormerod, "Structure of a Systematic Ecclesiology" 10.

20. Ben Meyer, *The Early Christians: Their World Mission and Self-Discovery* (Wilmington: Glazier, 1986) 23.

21. O'Malley, "Vatican II" 58.

22. Schloesser, "Against Forgetting" 96.

23. Notable works that have adopted this approach are Edward Schillebeeckx, *The Church with a Human Face: A New and Expanded Theology of Ministry* (New York: Crossroad, 1985); and David Bosch, *Transforming Mission: Paradigm Shifts in Theology of Mission* (Maryknoll, N.Y.: Orbis, 1991). Perhaps the most significant of recent attempts, if somewhat flawed in my opinion, is the work of Roger Haight, *Christian Community in History*, 2 vols. (New York: Continuum, 2004–2005). Haight's

work bears a superficial resemblance to the type of project Komonchak envisages. However, in my view, he severely underestimates the problems associated with bringing the social sciences into a theological project. His correlationist method is simply not adequate to the task. For details of my argument, see Ormerod, "Dialectic Engagement."

24. Walter Kasper, "A Friendly Reply to Cardinal Ratzinger on the Church," *America* 184 (April 23–30, 2001) 8–14. It is ironic that Kasper himself promotes a *communio* ecclesiology despite its idealistic overtones.

25. Frederick E. Crowe, *Lonergan*, Outstanding Christian Thinkers (Collegeville, Minn.: Liturgical, 1992) 22–23.

26. In Lonergan's terms this was an inverse insight, recognizing that there was no need to find an explanation for constant velocity. See Bernard J. F. Lonergan, *Insight: A Study of Human Understanding*, ed. Frederick E. Crowe and Robert M. Doran, Collected Works of Bernard Lonergan 3 (Toronto: University of Toronto, 1992) 43–50.

27. Bernard J. F. Lonergan, "Healing and Creating in History," in *A Third Collection*, ed. Frederick E. Crowe (Mahwah, N.J.: Paulist, 1985) 100–109.

28. Doran, *Theology and the Dialectics of History* 144.

29. Robert M. Doran, *What Is Systematic Theology?* (Toronto: University of Toronto, 2006) 62–66. Doran derives the terminology of a "unified field theory" from unpublished papers of Daniel Mansour.

30. See Neil J. Ormerod, "Quarrels with the Method of Correlation," *Theological Studies* 57 (1996) 707–19, for a more detailed analysis of this issue.

31. Ormerod, "Structure of a Systematic Ecclesiology" 19–20.

32. For a fuller treatment of the different styles of sociology and their theological significance, see Ormerod, "A Dialectic Engagement."

33. Christopher Dawson, *The Age of the Gods* (London: Sheed & Ward, 1933) xvi. Dawson lists his cases as A, B, C, etc., whereas I have enumerated them.

34. Ibid. xvi.

35. Ibid. xvii.
36. Ibid. xviii.
37. Ibid.
38. Ibid.
39. Ibid. xix.
40. Ibid. xvii.
41. Ibid.
42. Ibid. xviii.
43. As Komonchak notes ("Vatican II as an 'Event'" 37–39), historical judgments of an event such as Vatican II depend on how we identify them as an "episode in a plot."
44. O'Malley, "Vatican II" 88 n. 27; Schloesser, "Against Forgetting" 149 n. 109. Bernard J. F. Lonergan, "The Transition from a Classicist World-View to Historical Mindedness," in *A Second Collection*, ed. William F. Ryan and Bernard Tyrrell (Toronto: University of Toronto, 1996) 1–9.
45. This classicism is evident in the Apostolic Constitution of Benedict XV to the 1917 Code of Canon Law, where he states that the Church "promoted also most effectively the development of civilization. For not only did she abolish the laws of barbarous nations and remodel on more humane lines their savage customs, but likewise, with God's assistance, she reformed and brought to Christian perfection the very law of the Romans, that wonderful achievement of ancient wisdom" (Edward N. Peters, *The 1917 or Pio-Benedictine Code of Canon Law* [San Francisco: Ignatius, 2001] 21).
46. Neil J. Ormerod, "Church, Anti-Types, and Ordained Ministry," *Pacifica* 10 (1997) 331–49. In this article I had simply numbered the four antitypes that I now refer to as classic conservative, neo-conservative, semi-progressive, and totally progressive. As Komonchak observes ("Vatican II as an 'Event'" 43), the labels "progressive" and "conservative" are inadequate for the analysis of the Church, and indeed for any social context. The four antitypes add more nuance to these categorizations.
47. According to Peter L. Berger, *The Social Reality of Religion* (London: Faber, 1969) 166, "the sect, in its classical sociology-of-religion conception, serves as a model for organising a

cognitive minority *against* a hostile or at least non-believing milieu." The limitation of this conception lies in its failure to distinguish hostility at the cultural and social levels.

48. Schloesser, "Against Forgetting" 115–19, on the Church's rejection of modernity and its struggle to shift at Vatican II in the area of religious tolerance and pluralism.

49. The *nouvelle théologie* movement and the theologies of Rahner, Lonergan, and Doran are all attempts at overcoming the extrinsicism of neo-Scholasticism.

50. Dennis M. Doyle, *Communion Ecclesiology: Vision and Versions* (Maryknoll, N.Y.: Orbis, 2000) 41–42, on the ecclesiology of the manual tradition, which defines the final cause of the Church to be the beatific vision.

51. Schloesser, "Against Forgetting" 108–112, on the "Jewish question" as a context for Vatican II.

52. Perhaps the most notable example of this persistence is that of the tridentine seminary.

53. Dawson, *Age of the Gods* xvii–xviii.

54. Ormerod, "Structure of a Systematic Ecclesiology" 8–9.

55. *Redemptoris missio* no.15, http://www.vatican.va/holy_father/ john_paul_ii/encyclicals/documents/hf_jp-ii_enc_07121990_ redemptoris-missio_en.html (accessed August 7, 2006, emphasis added).

56. Quoted in Schloesser, "Against Forgetting" 107.

57. John Allen, "Weigel Puts Favorable Spin on John Paul's Pontificate," *National Catholic Reporter* 36.3 (November 5, 1999) 37.

58. See the works of Alasdair MacIntyre, *Whose Justice? Which Rationality?* (Notre Dame, Ind.: University of Notre Dame, 1988); Alasdair MacIntyre, *Three Rival Versions of Moral Enquiry: Encyclopaedia, Genealogy, and Tradition: Being Gifford Lectures Delivered in the University of Edinburgh in 1988* (Notre Dame, Ind.: University of Notre Dame, 1990).

59. See, Neil J. Ormerod, "New Age: Threat or Opportunity," *Australasian Catholic Record* 71 (1994) 74–81, where I argue that the New Age movement represents such a compensatory stance toward cosmological symbolism.

60. Bjørnar Olsen, "The End of History? Archaeology and the Politics of Identity in a Globalized World," in *The Destruction and Conservation of Cultural Property*, ed. Robert Layton et al. (New York: Routledge, 2001) 47 notes: "On the other hand we can identify a completely opposed reaction [to globalization] in many parts of the world: cultural and religious fundamentalism, neo-nationalism, and the increasing ethnification of the political discourse, in short what Friedman has referred to as the 'Balkanisation and tribalisation experienced at the bottom of the system' (Friedman 1997:85). In the wake of this we see the proliferation of myths of origins and authenticity, and how the past increasingly is being used as a foundation for 'histories of revenge'. The latter reaction, and the way the past is being used in 'defence' of existing or invented identities, may remind us that what we are facing is as much the 'return' of history as the end of it. The resurgence of ethnic nationalism in Europe and elsewhere has given hundreds of historians full-time occupation in writing glorious histories for their peoples. As noted by Eriksen, . . . 'It is never too late to have a happy childhood.'"

61. One thinks of the great social encyclicals of John Paul II, such as *Laborens exercens* (1981), *Solicitudo rei socialis* (1987), and *Centesimus annus* (1991).

62. For an analysis of globalization using these same tools, see Neil J. Ormerod, "Theology, History, and Globalization," *Gregorianum* 88 (2007) 23–48.

63. The process of change had been going on behind the scenes since the condemnation of "Modernism" in 1907. One thinks of major contributions in the first half of the 20th century made by theologians who eventually served as periti at the council such as Karl Rahner, Henri de Lubac, Edward Schillebeeckx, Yves Congar, Hans Küng, and John Courtney Murray, and liturgiologists like Odo Casel and Josef Jungmann.

64. One thinks of names such as Charles Curran, Edward Schillebeeckx, Roger Haight, Leonardo Boff, Anthony de Mello, Jacques Dupuis, together with documents such as Instruction on Christian Freedom and Liberation (1986), *Dominus Iesus* (2000), and the overarching document, Instruction on the

Ecclesial Vocation of the Theologian (1990). One should also refer to a number of encyclicals of John Paul II on moral questions, such as *Veritatis splendor* (1993), *Evangelium vitae* (1995), and the apostolic letter on the nonordination of women, *Ordinatio sacerdotalis* (1994).

65. Lonergan, *Method in Theology* xi.
66. Ibid. 320–24. See also Doran, *What Is Systematic Theology?* 133–36, on the distinction between understanding data and understanding facts. In relation to issues in trinitarian theology see Neil J. Ormerod, *Trinity: Retrieving the Western Tradition* (Milwaukee: Marquette University, 2005) 143–52.
67. Ormerod, "Structure of a Systematic Ecclesiology" 27–29.
68. Schloesser makes the same observation about repeated calls for unity in the documents of Vatican II themselves ("Against Forgetting" 96–97).
69. *Instrumentum laboris* of the 2001 Synod of Bishops, The Bishop: Servant of the Gospel of Jesus Christ for the Hope of the World no. 62, http://www.vatican.va/roman_curia/synod/documents/rc_synod_doc_20010601_instrumentum-laboris_en.html (accessed August 7, 2006). Significantly, on six occasions where the document links "communion" and "mission," it does so with an explicitly trinitarian dimension.
70. As *Redemptoris missio* notes, "the Church is missionary by her very nature" (no. 5).
71. As O'Malley observes, these key notions of the council "are both geared to change" (O'Malley, "Vatican II" 63).
72. *Redemptoris missio* no.15.
73. An earlier draft of this article was presented at the 33rd Annual Lonergan Workshop at Boston College, June 2006.

CONTRIBUTORS

JOSEPH A. KOMONCHAK received his licentiate in theology from the Gregorian University in Rome and his Ph.D. in philosophy from Union Theological Seminary, New York. He now holds the John and Gertrude Hubbard Chair in Religious Studies at the Catholic University of America. His primary interests include the history and theology of Vatican II, ecclesiology, and modern theology. A prolific author, he teamed with Giuseppe Alberigo in editing the monumental *History of Vatican II* (Orbis 1995–2006).

JOHN W. O'MALLEY, S.J., received his Ph.D. from Harvard University and is now University Professor at Georgetown University. He has published widely in the area of 16th-century religious culture, most recently his acclaimed, *Four Cultures of the West* (Harvard University, 2004). He has also recently edited two volumes, *The Jesuits and the Arts*, 1540–1773 (St. Joseph's University, 2005) and *The Jesuits II: Cultures, Sciences, and the Arts, 1540–1773* (University of Toronto, 2006). Next summer Harvard University Press will publish his monograph on Vatican II.

NEIL J. ORMEROD holds a D.Theol. from Melbourne College of Divinity and a Ph.D. in pure mathematics from the University of New South Wales. He is professor of theology at Australian Catholic University, Strathfield, N.S.W., and director of the Institute of Theology, Philosophy, and Religious Education. Focusing on Lonergan studies, trinitarian theology, ecclesiology, and the relationship between theology and the social sciences, his most recent publications include: *Creation, Grace, and Redemption* (Orbis, 2007) and "Theology, History, and Globalization," *Gregorianum* 88 (2007). In progress is a monograph with Shane Clifton entitled "Globalization and the Mission of the Church."

STEPHEN SCHLOESSER, S.J., having earned his Ph.D. in History and Humanities at Stanford University, is an associate professor of history at Boston College and adjunct associate professor at Weston Jesuit School of Theology in Cambridge, Mass. His area of special competence is late modern Europe (1789 to the present) with a focus on France. His *Jazz Age Catholicism: Mystic Modernism in Postwar Paris, 1919–1933* (University of Toronto, 2005) received the American Catholic Historical Association's John Gilmary Shea Prize for the most original and distinguished contribution to knowledge of the history of the Catholic Church. In process are a monograph— *Visions of Amen: Olivier Messiaen, Catholic Revivalism, Mystic Modernism* (Eerdmans)—and an art exhibition: *Mystic Masque: Semblance and Reality in Georges Rouault, 1871–1958.*

DAVID G. SCHULTENOVER, S.J., received his Ph.D. in historical theology from St. Louis University and is now professor of historical theology in the Department of Theology at Marquette University. Since 2006 he also serves as the editor in chief of *Theological Studies*. His primary interests are Roman Catholic Modernism, nineteenth-century Continental theology, and the use of anthropology in the study of history. His recent publications include: "Luis Martín García (1846–1906), the Jesuit General of the Modernist Crisis: On Historical Criticism," *Catholic Historical Review* (July 2003), and the edited collection *The Reception of Pragmatism in France and the Rise of Catholic Modernism, 1890–1914* (Catholic University of America, 2008). In process is a book-length biographical study of Luis Martín.